D0340926

SPORTS CARD COLLECTOR 101

THE SIMPLIFIED NEWBIE'S GUIDE TO START COLLECTING AND INVESTING IN SPORTS CARDS IN LESS THAN 7 DAYS

BETO SALINAS

Interior Design by FormattedBooks.com

CONTENTS

How to get $98 worth of Sports Cards Research for Free

Free Bonus #1 ($49 value)

"7 Things You Must Do Before
Buying A Sports Card"

Free Bonus #2 ($49 value)

Our Custom Spreadsheet To Help You
Visualize The Price Trending And Projections
Of Your Favorite Sports Cards.

To get your Bonuses go to
https://betosalinas.activehosted.com/f/1

THE EVOLUTION OF SPORTS CARD COLLECTING

"Oh hell, who wants to collect that crap?"
—Babe Ruth, on collecting autographs.

Enter one of the most exciting hobbies for the new age. It might come as a surprise to you that this fascinating pastime happened quite by accident!

If you are a smoker, you might be familiar with Tobacconist James Buchanan Duke's story, otherwise known as "Buck" (yes, this is the same Buck from Duke University). Towards the pinnacle of the 19th century, he decided to put small sheets of cardboard into his packs of smokes to both stiffen the package, allowing it to maintain its perfect rectangular form and protect the cigarettes while in transit. Ingenious, don't you think?

The one side of the card was used for advertising purposes from the manufacturer, and the flip side was an eagerly anticipated event for every smoker. You see, on the other side of that cardboard was the picture of a well-known actor.

Buchanan's rivals were so taken with this revolutionary marketing idea that they copied it and started producing cardboard sheets of a similar nature and began using photos from other celebrities in their packs of cigarettes. The cards that championed that era's baseball stars are the true heroes of this story since they are ultimately the catalysts of this invention and gained widespread popularity amongst the "accidental collectors."

Sadly, the early 1900s saw the production of sports cards plummeting. This is due to Camel cigarettes entering the market, together with the R.J. Reynolds Company's arrival. R.J Reynolds launched a campaign warning their consumers not to "look for premiums or coupons, as the cost of the tobacco blended in CAMEL Cigarettes prohibits the use of them." This statement saw nearly every other tobacco manufacturer cease the production of sports cards in fear of being labeled as inferior to CAMEL.

Just when sports card collecting enthusiasts thought that this might be the end of their newfound hobby, it rose from the fire like a phoenix! This resurgence occurred in the mid-20th century, this time by bubble gum manufacturers. Rival bubble gum companies became competitive with one another to gain consumer popularity.

In that era, the two top competitors were Topps Chewing Gum and Bowman Gum Company; they remained top of their game by signing football and baseball's biggest names.

In 1956, Topps became top of the log when they took ownership of the Bowman company. The following 25 years saw them dominate the baseball card industry and maintaining exclusivity over football cards between 1956 and 1988.

Their reign came to a grinding halt in 1981 after losing an antitrust suit filed by the Fleer Corporation. The time period of 1956–1980 for baseball cards and 1956–1988 has forever been etched as the "Topps Era" in the card collecting community.

The Kellogg's Sports Cards

Many of our seasoned sports cards collectors will fondly recall the excitement of tearing open a new box of cereal from the Kellogg's range in pursuit of (hopefully) a new sports card to add to our growing collection.

If you were a family of a few kids, much debate and negotiation had to incur to decide who the lucky recipient was to be when Mom needed to play referee. The excitement was elevated to a new height as you had to submerge your hand into the crunchy cereal in search of your treasure.

The toothy grin was always an indication of what was to come when the debating contest winner pulled out their hand to reveal a shiny 3D card to their peers. Forty years on, many sports card enthusiasts still fondly hold on to their now-vintage 3D sports card that they had so proudly gathered and kept close to their hearts.

How many boxes of cereal did we consume during the 70s and '80s? We will never forget those special mornings and the feeling of childhood sentimentality that accompanies those whimsical recollections. Today, we still collect them, both as a reminder of our innocence and as the rarity that they represent today.

Companies, such as Professional Sports Authenticator (PSA), are widely respected for their gameplay in grading cards. They assign a grade to a collectible card and then place it in the confines of a plastic holder.

Many of the Ratz 3D cards are graded in a near-Mint or a higher equivalent, and Kellogg's cards from 1971 are knighted with PSA's highest possible grade of a 10 (implying a Gem Mint condition). Having these in your collection can make you a collector with value in your back pocket.

For example, in 2008, Kellogg's PSA 10's of quarterback Gary Cuozzo, a non-star player and football legend Dick Butkus, 1971, were auctioned and bought for about $640 and $1,200, respectively. In PSA 8 (Near-Mint) condition, they currently list for $8 and $30, in comparison.

In 2005, a 1971 Kellogg's PSA 10 of Roberto Clemente sold for close to $1,500. In PSA 8, that sports card of the baseball icon currently lists at approximately $75.

With their intricate layers of protective plastic, the question is asked on how do they then perform in that capsule? It is a rare occasion when a Kellogg's card breaks in a holder that has been graded professionally (1/100 to be precise).

The general rule of thumb is that, if the cardholder does not manifest any flaws after it has been encased 40 years earlier, it is viewed as a sports card of immense value. If it doesn't show any flaws after 40 years, it is precious.

The only exception to this rule is when it is exposed to extreme elements and/or conditions; this, alone, implies that you are rest assured of your investment in the long-run.

Its current strength of baseball cards originates from America's revived love affair with baseball as a sport in this decade. It is important to note that card manufacturers aren't very mindful of either recessions or booming times.

Much of their revenue has been generated from the booming market demand for vintage baseball cards; this was classified as a secondary market that produced $500 million in sales in recent years. Who is their niche market? Seven to 12-year-olds! And these little ones are the determining factor as to whether the baseball card manufacturers will be profitable or not.

Previously sports card manufacturers reckoned that between 75% and 90% of their sales were from kids. Nowadays, it is us older "kids" that are collecting sports cards at breakneck speed.

A Word From the Author

Before we embark on our journey, we have to state that, in order to keep the price of this book at a minimum, we have decided to print it in black-and-white. But to make it even better, we have decided to create a website and pdf document with the pictures in color and the color variations of some sets.

— CHAPTER 1 —

DRUM ROLL PLEASE - A FORMAL INTRODUCTION

"Every time I sign a ball, and there must have been thousands, I thank my luck that I wasn't born Coveleski or Wambsganss or Peckinpaugh." —Mel Ott, New York Giants.

The whole dog and pony show should accompany this introductory drum roll. Nothing can prepare you for the exciting adventure on which you are about to embark.

Trust us when we say you will walk away from this book (and keep coming back to it) with a complete guide of all the information you need to know for you to become a fully-fledged sports card collecting fundi. A fundi is a person who has extensive knowledge about a certain topic.

WORLD OF SPORTS CARD COLLECTING

Superior to Fantasy Leagues

Yes, you read, right! We are entering into this chapter with a bold statement by saying that sports card collecting is a superior version of fantasy leagues. Why is this, you ask?

Naturally, fantasy league enthusiasts will agree that this concept goes hand-in-hand with sports card collecting.

Our opinion as the author of this book is that the fantasy league option allows you to freely pick your players of choice in the hopes of them performing well during the sports season.

In reality, you will then collect the sports card of the favorite players, but instead of hoping for them to earn points to their name, you secretly hope that they perform at their peak. This will naturally increase the value of your sports card collection.

For example, in the fantasy football leagues, there is an emphasis on the weekly games played. With sports card collecting, it is about how they perform on-field as well as off-field.

In fantasy league terms, if the player is part of the championship-winning team or the golden child that has contributed the most points, it is irrelevant whether they have an accomplished season.

In the hemisphere of sports card collection, winning the championship increases the value of your sports card collection.

Another critical difference between the two is that if a player makes it to the all-star gaming league or is cited as the Most Valuable Player (MVP for short), it bears very little to no effect at all.

Again, in sports card collecting terms, if your player makes it to the all-star game or pro-bowl league, this escalates your sports card price value. Should your player partake in any unfavorable activities off-field, such as saying something controversial in an interview, this won't affect the tour fantasy league's outcome but will negatively impact your card's worth.

In conclusion, fantasy league games and sports card collecting go hand-in-hand but, in our opinion, sports cards go way beyond how players perform on the field on a weekly basis.

When your player is injured in the fantasy league, you have the option of replacing them with an uninjured player as an alternative. In sports cards, not only does it impact your sports card's value, you have to make an important decision as to whether you are going to hold on to that card (hoping that the player returns soon and plays well), or you will have to settle in selling the sports card in question for a lower price.

Collecting vs. Investing

You need to ask yourself whether you are a collector of or investor in sports cards. But, there is no harm in playing both sides of the field on this one.

This is a personal choice, and there really is no right or wrong way to go about it. The individuals who are more concerned with sports card investing have been known to make a considerable amount of capital from their investments in the last decade.

In the last five years alone, the prices of sports cards have increased dramatically. This includes both the selling and the purchase price.

For investors to make that all-important executive decision, they use all of the sales performance tools in their arsenal before executing a purchase of any kind. Some of these trading techniques include the price (buying or selling) of a particular sports card, from a specific reputable brand, at an indicated time.

Many individuals refer to the sports card collecting initiative as merely a hobby. Even though it can quite rightly be categorized as such, others take it to the next level and fully embrace it as an investment.

If you are looking to make some money from it, you will naturally fall in the latter category. Serious investors spend many hours online, conducting research and then applying it in practice.

Should you decide to pursue sports card collecting as an investment, you need to look at it from a trader's perspective. It is similar to an individual who monitors the stock exchange regularly (if not on a daily) basis.

You should have in-depth insights into the diversity of your portfolio in its entirety. Hardcore traders ensure that they never miss out on the perfect opportunity to buy or sell their sports cards. This implies checking statistics frequently.

It begs the question that, if you are not doing this, are you then classified as a collector instead? To be classified as active in the investment game, you need to do thorough online research on eBay, Facebook, and even Instagram.

It is not our place to force to maintain a diverse portfolio. But, to use an example, a 1986 Michael Jordan RC graded at PSA nine four years ago, and you would have forked out more or less \$3000–\$3500, depending on where the card was purchased. Recently, that card has sold for \$6000–\$6500.

This means that, four years ago, you could've had not only a blue-chip in your collection or portfolio, but you could've had triple the returns in investment. For this particular card, the Jordan era will always be relevant, meaning that the card's value will be on the rise even more.

We believe that all collections or portfolios should possess at least one blue-chip card in their inventory. This sports card type forms a sort of security in that it can be liquidated easily as a means of backup.

Once you get your hands on such a card, you can then delve into minor cards and extend this to various other sports types. From there, you will continue to invest in these minor cards from a multitude of sport disciplines until you reach several sports cards that are comfortable for you to manage.

There should be a clear distinction between cards for investment purposes and sports cards for collection purposes. This will ensure that you can compartmentalize between cards that can be held or sold for a profit.

A big issue when it comes to sports card investing is that time is not your friend. You might find it extremely challenging to manage your time. The best way to mitigate this is to find a system that works for you and not the other way around.

Sports card investing is a volatile market that is greatly influenced by an array of factors that can either increase or decrease a card's price. It is best to try, as far as possible, to check the news daily on events that can influence the value of the cards you hold in your hand.

Even though you might consider doing this on a serious investor level, you should always remember to have fun. Trading sports cards for investment purposes should still be pleasurable!

Rookie Cards for the Win

We recommend only buying/collecting/or investing in rookie sports cards. The reason for this is because rookie cards will hold their value better than the other sports cards in your portfolio.

Rookie cards can't be exploited or manipulated. Even when a new card is released, the rookie card will remain intact. Your aim as a collector or investor is to obtain the player's first card ever published in question. This is also referred to as the rookie card.

In the instance of the rookie card becoming too costly to purchase, buyers will instead show a preference in the same player's second or third-year sports cards. As an example, LeBron James' first Miami Heat card trades for $2.5k+ now.

In the case of the Memphis Grizzlies' #12 (point guard) Mr. Ja Morant's, a significant portion of the graded card listings were 2019 Panini Prizm—implying that this is his main rookie card.

Panini Prizm or Topps Chrome will typically be the primary rookie card sets for some of the more recent players. Panini gained the exclusive NBA license for sports trading cards in the 2009–2010 season.

For LA Lakers' LeBron James, his rookie card is the 2003 Topps Chrome. And for Giannis Antetokounpo, his rookie card is from the 2013 Panini Prizm Basketball box set.

When buying on eBay, you can scroll through and start to get a feel for the prices. The rookie card is usually the most desirable by buyers. It will subsequently be the first card to increase in value relating to the player's performance and future prospects, if this fits within your budgetary calculations.

When applying the calculations, it is best to take the average of the last five sales transactions and use that to determine a fair price. Bear in mind that, when you sell on platforms eBay or StockX, there is a -13% fee for the seller.

This means that, when you are buying from an individual directly, you can expect the prices to be anywhere between 10%–15% less than to be paid on an online platform.

The next factor to consider is all the associated variables determining whether the sports card is an excellent short- or long-term investment. Factors that influence this are:

- The sports card grade.
- The population report (pop report). This refers to the accounting of the cards the companies have graded.
- The artwork on the card, etc.

The Exception to the Rookie Card Rule

We already established that the art of sports card collecting is making a retro comeback. The only exception to the Rookie card rule would be to invest in a sports card of a sporting great such as Lebron James, Kobe Bryant, etc.

It has been projected that, in the next few decades, sports cards like those mentioned above—referred to as the "emerging classics"—will experience a sharp spike in sales and interest.

Over time, the best possible investment will be those sports stars that are seen as icons in their respective disciplines. This will happen gradually. Many sports card enthusiasts, especially the newbies, will focus their sights in the first three years and invest in the newer sports stars.

If this is the approach that you are planning on following, then it is suggested to flip the cards in the next two years instead of holding on to them for the next ten years. In essence, the rookie card is unique in that there is only one card of this year, vs. the average career span and card reprints of the five to 15-year mark.

The Market Demand for Sports Cards

In an era when we are fighting a battle against a worldwide pandemic, the hobby of sports card collection has been in serious incline.

Cards of sporting legends, such as Michael Jordan, have recorded many sales records. Lebron James' 2019-2020 base Prizm PSA 10 cards currently trade upwards of $200. A crucial factor to bear in mind is knowing when to sell which sports cards. Failure to do so can result in either selling valuable cards too soon or buying cards that hold little value.

The current total market value of the sports card fraternity is estimated to be worth 5.4 billion dollars. This figure was calculated by tech entrepreneur David Yoken as cited by Forbes magazine in an online article.

This calculation was based on "the total Gross Merchandise Volume (GMV) from eBay, independent auction houses, online retail venues, and other sources." eBay contributed a total of $4.7 billion to the sales.

It has to be mentioned that the data gathered from eBay is not 100% accurate as the platform does not share clear-cut sales data. But the information that is supplied can act as a guide for buyers and sellers alike.

eBay is only one of many sources of sales information. Other platforms, such as Facebook Marketplace and the many sports card trading groups, are also information-rich on this topic.

On Facebook alone, you can expect to see over 30,000 sports card enthusiasts posting a total number of 6,000 times on these groups. The estimated amount of $5.4 billion market size is highly likely to be too low.

Compare it to products of a similar nature, such as sneaker flipping, art, and the art of coin collecting. They are rated and valued using the same principles, such as cosmetic or aesthetic value, how rare they are, and if there is a demand for the collection.

- The coin market alone (except for silver and gold bullion) is currently valued at a market worth of $4 billion.
- The art market on a global scale is currently valued at $64 billion.
- The flipping of sneakers is estimated to be worth $2 billion, and it is projected to grow triple in size.

What are the Prospects for the Sports Card Hemisphere?

There is no credible source yet, but serious sports card collectors and investors are adamant that the market has not yet reached its pinnacle. Some factors that indicate the veracity of this statement include:

The Ratio of Awareness

Jonathan Torrey, a blogger from the Sports Card Investor website, has conducted an interesting theory in that one out of every 50 people currently trade in sports cards. This implies that the majority of the world has not yet become aware of this global phenomenon.

Facebook Outreach

Jonathan also conducted a faux campaign to determine the interest in the sports card market and gained valuable insights on the prospective future demand.

He received data that indicated that approximately 1.5 million individuals worldwide had expressed their interest in sports memorabilia on the platform. When this data is utilized, it is estimated that the average sports enthusiast spends $3,600 on various sports merchandise and collectibles.

It is important to note that the assumed spending per person is not set in stone, but it will give a good indication. Due to the cost of data and other factors, such as internet accessibility in third-world countries, many people are not even aware of Facebook, much less sports cards collecting and/or investing.

The Social Media "CCTV Cameras"

This is the term of endearment we have coined for the die-hard social media followers of sports icons such as Lebron James. It might come as a complete surprise that the Louvre art museum in Paris is what Lebron is to the basketball world. Yes, you guessed it!

James currently has 65.9 million followers on Instagram, and the Louvre (one of the most popular tourist destinations in the world) only has 4 million.

Most people might think that the trading price for one of Lebron's rookie cards is too high (the current price is $7,000), but there are only 1988 PSA 10 Topps Chrome cards of this kind in circulation.

To put it in context, if each of James' Instagram followers wanted to purchase one of his rookie cards, there are only 0.00003% that can possibly own one of them. And he doesn't even have the most followers on this platform.

In an ideal world, if only .25% of Lebron's following had $7,000 disposable income they could spend, 302,500 followers would be in competition to get one of these sought-after rookie cards. This means that sellers are in the driving seat, and the demand will increase dramatically over time, as previously discussed.

How to Determine Your Reason for This Hobby

Seasoned sports card collectors and investors who are actively pursuing this initiative have experienced that the 2021 version vs. the 80s and 90s way of doing things are entirely different.

Therefore, the hobby has evolved and is a much more complicated process compared to your innocent days when you did not know any better, and you just wanted as many sports cards as possible. You would then trade this amongst your friends and cousins.

Finding your *why* in this hobby will arm you with the crucial data that will flow over to the *how's* and the *what's*. When starting, you might feel completely overwhelmed by all the in's and out's.

When you have determined the purpose of your portfolio, proverbially speaking, all the sports cards will then fall into place. This way, you will also be able to drown out the noise and know which information is relevant to your goal.

Performing your due diligence in this regard will help you to make the right decisions at the right time and stop you from possibly overspending out of fear, only to see the cards you bought the night before dropping dramatically in price the next day. In the end, you don't want to sit with buyer's remorse, which would take the fun out of what you are doing.

Above all else, this needs to be a memorable experience for you.

THE TOP SELLING SPORTS CARDS ON THE MARKET

Baseball

Number: 1
Card name: 1909 *T206* Honus Wagner
Year sold: 2016
Selling price: $3.12 million
Number: 2
Card name: 1952 *Topps* Mickey Mantle
Year sold: 2018
Selling price: $2.88 million
Number: 3
Card name: 1951 *Bowman* Mickey Mantle
Year sold: 2018
Selling price: $750,000
Number: 4
Card name: 1916 *Sporting News* Babe Ruth
Year sold: 2016
Selling price: $717,000
Number: 5
Card name: 1963 *Topps* Pete Rose
Year sold: 2016
Selling price: $717,000

Baseball

Number: 1
Card name: 1909 *T206* Honus Wagner
Year sold: 2016
Selling price: $3.12 million

Number: 2
Card name: 1952 *Topps* Mickey Mantle
Year sold: 2018
Selling price: $2.88 million
Number: 3
Card name: 1951 *Bowman* Mickey Mantle
Year sold: 2018
Selling price: $750,000
Number: 4
Card name: 1916 *Sporting News* Babe Ruth
Year sold: 2016
Selling price: $717,000
Number: 5
Card name: 1963 *Topps* Pete Rose
Year sold: 2016
Selling price: $717,000

Basketball

Number: 1
Card name: 2013–2014 *Panini* Giannis Antetokounmpo
Year sold: 2020
Selling price: $1,857,300
Number: 2
Card name: 2003–2004 *Upper Deck* Lebron James
Year sold: 2020
Selling price: $1,845,000
Number: 3
Card name: 2003–2004 *Upper Deck* Michael Jordan
Year sold: 2020
Selling price: $900,000
Number: 4

Card name: 1969–1970 *Topps* Kareem Abdul-Jabbar (formerly known as Lew Alcindor)
Year sold: 2020
Selling price: $534,678
Number: 5
Card name: 1948 *Bowman* George Mikan
Year sold: 2020
Selling price: $435,399

American Football

Number: 1
Card name: 1935 National Chicle – Bronko Nagurski (RC)
Grading: PSA 9 – Mint
Estimated value: $750,000
Number: 2
Card name: 1948 Leaf – Bobby Layne (RC)
Grading: PSA 9 – Mint
Estimated value: $45,000
Number: 3
Card name: 1948 Leaf – Chuck Bednarik (RC)
Grading: PSA 9 – Mint
Estimated value: $30,000
Number: 4
Card name: 1894 N302 Mayo's Cut Plug- John Dunlop
Grading: PSA 3, VG
Estimated value: $22,750
Number: 5
Card name: 1935 National Chicle – Knute Rockne
Grading: PSA 9 – Mint
Estimated value: $16,500

Hockey

Number: 1
Card name: 1979 *O-Pee-Chee* Wayne Gretzky
Estimated value: $50,000
Number: 2
Card name: 1966 *Topps* Bobby Orr
Estimated value: $40,000
Number: 3
Card name: 1951 *Parkhurst* Gordie Howe
Estimated value: $40,000
Number: 4
Card name: 1990-91 *O-Pee-Cee* Premier Maurice Richard
Estimated value: $15,000
Number: 5
Card name: 1985 *Topps* Mario Lemieux
Estimated value: $14,000

INSERT CARDS OR CHASE CARDS

Base Cards

Many people ask if beauty can be measured. Our response to this is that when it comes to sports cards, you can!

An insert card is a card that is randomly placed in a pack of sports cards. Insert cards or chase cards do not form part of the standard base set's numbering system. They also tend to have a design that differs from the rest of the pack.

Instead, they form part of a set within a set or can be a "subset" on their own. They look entirely different and also have another naming convention.

As we have already discussed, rookie cards hold value as they are the first year of production for a player and cannot be forged as a different year. This factor makes them rare.

Brands, such as Optic and Prizm, have become legends in their own right, and this makes the sports card collectors hold on to these cards in the same way they hold on to their rookie cards.

Due to these cards' exponential growth, we advise every newbie sports card collector to add Optic and Prizm rookie cards to their collection as soon as possible, while the trend is on the incline.

In their efforts to obtain Prizms, Optics, etc., many investors and collectors seemingly overlook base cards' value as they are after the big guns.

They might not be the primary sports cards to buy, but they do have their place in your portfolio. Investing in base cards can afford a collector the opportunity to earn some money to purchase cards of a higher rank and value.

The question to ask yourself is, do you buy these lower-end cards to earn money or strengthen the value of your portfolio?

Chase Cards

These are cards from sets that are used as a substitute for an insert card by entertainment companies or non-sport trading card manufacturers.

Jerseys

A Jersey card is a sports card that contains a piece of that particular player's kit or uniform. It might be an affordable option to own a piece of material used in a game but cannot afford the full jersey.

This notion transforms the sports card collecting hemisphere into a series of stackable Matryoshka Dolls. One type of sports card craze is used to manufacture another one, just like the Russian nesting dolls.

These game-used jersey cards are the genius of manufacturer *Upper Deck*. *Upper Deck* was the first manufacturer to introduce these cards to the world in 1996, with their UD Game Set.

Suddenly, it was not just about holding a piece of cardboard with a picture on the front, but an actual tangible object that touched your sports idol! Initially, the '96 UD Game Set was very popular, but it has become widespread amongst sport card enthusiasts since then.

The "in" thing right now is a player's Rookie Patch Autograph (RPA). This features their rookie card, a piece of their kit (generally with the color and a part of their number), plus their autograph. These sports cards can be high in value with the combination of the rookie card and their autograph dynamic.

Jersey cards are also sometimes referred to as Patch cards.

Memorabilia

The same concept has also extended to other sport player memorabilia. To date, other items such as:

- Bats
- Balls
- Buttons
- Caps

- Dirt (yes, you read right)
- Field or turf grass
- Helmets
- Pants
- Pitch base pieces
- Gloves
- Shoes
- Shoelaces
- Stadium seats
- and even eye black stickers

have been added to sports cards. It is questionable as to whether these pieces are from actual game days. The increase in the demand for these items has forced manufacturers to get creative and use memorabilia signed at premiere signing events.

The most peculiar instance of memorabilia that is going to be used to print sports cards is Manny Machados' introductory presser table tablecloth.

The origin of the material also plays an integral part in the price. For instance, if the fabric used forms part of a tag, patch, or league logo, it is regarded more valuable than a plain jersey where specific marks of identification have been omitted.

Autographed Sports Cards

There are different types of autographed sports cards; these include:

Autographed card

This is a card that has been signed by the player. This is classified as a certified autograph.

Hard-signed autographed card
This refers to an autographed card where the player's signature has been inscribed onto the card's surface.

Label or Sticker autographed card
This is also an autographed card with a certified signature on a clear label and attached to the sports card's surface during the production phase.

Rookie Cards

This is a base card (non-parallel version) released in their first year or a card made in the rookie's first year in the sports.

These are extremely valuable as the card can never be reprinted again, and they are incredibly scarce.

Parallels

This term speaks of a card that has been allocated a serial number and is part of a different card that has not been allotted a serial number.

An example would be that a base card is unnumbered, but the parallel version of that same card will be given a serial number.

Parallels typically have the same picture or design elements but in different colors.

Buy Back Cards

The 90s saw sports card manufacturer *Upper Deck* buying back their own cards. The aim of this was so that they could then put these cards back into circulation in their current products at the time.

When they get the card back, they would get the sports star to sign them and put them back into another product. These are referred to as buy-back autographed cards. They get a unique hologram from the *Upper Deck* Authentication program, and it comes with a certificate to confirm its authenticity.

Decoy Cards

Naturally, some collectors want to take a shortcut when it comes to sports card collecting. Some packs contain randomly inserted cards of great value.

They enter retail stores and spend hours performing an act called "pack searching." They would pour over the cards, feeling through the foil packaging, and weigh the packs to see if there are weight differences. This way, they can tell apart the packets that contain rare cards from those that don't.

This is a very dishonest and unfair practice towards other collectors. The antics they employ get more creative by the day. As a result, manufacturers are employing some innovative tactics of their own. They have now resorted to putting decoy cards in an attempt to trick the tricksters. It feels just like the real McCoy!

The e|Card

This is a unique offering from sports card producer *Upper Deck*. Enter the age of the e|card. This is a sports card with dynamic virtual capabilities. Every card is printed with a distinguishing serial number and adds to its collectability.

Sports card collectors are given access to their very own digital collection. If that serial number is entered, it takes you to a virtual platform. You can have as many cards in your digital collection as you can find.

When you enter the serial numbers, a thumbnail image appears at the lower part of your PC, giving you a mini slide show of your collection.

As you browse through your portfolio, you can choose any one of your cards. You are then provided with a full-sized version. What is so remarkable about this project is that your card can (you guessed it) e|volve into an upgraded version. It is as simple as selecting one of your digital cards and checking to see if it now classifies as an upgraded card.

In the case that it does not e|volve, you will be given access to a bonus picture of your athlete. The card will stay in your virtual portfolio, and the chance of it e|volving also remains a possibility.

e|cards can also transform into an autographed card, a game-used memorabilia card, or even a signed version of the latter, series depending. When you get lucky and your card e|volves, you will be taken to a page where you will complete your personal info, and your new e|volved card will be sent to your address.

Redemption Cards

In some instances, the sports card maker will insert a trade card or redemption card in the place of another article. This card can be sent to the manufacturer, and they will send you the article.

In most cases, these cards can be traded for articles that can't fit into the packs. Perhaps an autographed ball, now that can't fit into a pack, right?

Another type of trade card might also direct collector traffic to the website of the manufacturer. The aim is for the collector to view the article they can redeem the card for, which will be sent to them.

This is great from a digital aspect, as the collector then does not have to actually snail mail their card to the manufacturer. *Upper Deck* are the pioneers of this technology.

Upper Deck and its counterparts don't always have the inventory on hand offered on the trading card and add an expiration date on the redemption card. If you find yourself in this scenario where the item you can redeem your card for is out of stock, or if you missed the redemption deadline, you can contact the manufacturer to enquire if you can still redeem the card or whether they can send you a replacement card.

THE PRICE COMPONENTS OF A SPORTS CARD

Many factors determine the price or value of a sports card. These include:

Player or Team

The more famous the team or the player, the more attractive the card will be. The cards of Hall of Famers, such as Mickey Mantle, Mike Trout, Mookie Betts, Jackie Robinson, or Cody Bellinger, will be more valuable than their less-famous counterparts.

Similarly, this will be the case for teams too. When it comes to teams, such as the 27-time World Series Champions, the New York Yankees are extremely attractive to investors and collectors for this very reason.

For teams that do not perform as well, the allure of their cards might not be as pleasing, except in the case of someone like Tony Gwynn.

The sentimentality factor doesn't normally add to a card's value on a big scale. But the cards of the sports icons will generally be of higher value than the rest, especially in the case of their rookie cards. This is the very first year that is representative of league-licensed releases and is very dear to the collectors.

Condition of the Sports Card

The state of the card you purchase will be the most crucial of all the factors to consider.

A card in mint or near mint condition will always be more valuable than a card in a poor state.

It won't matter how rare the card is. If it is in a poor state, this will negatively affect the value of a card.

The state of the card is categorized by the following factors and the wear and tear thereof:

Corners

The corners should retain their sharp, well-formed edges. If the corners of the cards are torn or bent, this will drop the card's value.

Edges

The edges of the sports card should not have any dents or chips in them. You can assess this by turning the card sideways in a lit room and checking for any potential damage.

Centering

What is implied with this term is how the image was printed on the sports card. The PSA determines the card's centering by measuring the borders from left to right and then again from top to bottom.

The border should have a 50/50 width on all four of its sides. The more off-centered the card is, the more it will affect the grading and value thereof.

Surfaces

Sports cards can have many different surfaces. These include shiny or metallic finishes. This makes it easily distinguishable from any form of damage and can be seen by the eye.

A sports card with a suitable surface will be free from marks, will not have faded, or be stained in any way.

Scarcity

Before the 80s, sports cards were rarely manufactured. Due to this, some cards will be higher in value due to their rarity and age. Cards that were produced after this period might often be of a lower value than their counterparts.

Higher numbered cards printed in the respective sports series toward the end of the baseball seasons were extremely difficult to obtain and considered of higher worth. They might even sell for more than an earlier series.

There is a series that is referred to as "short prints." This means that a limited number of these cards were printed and are seldomly available for purchase. This makes them extremely valuable to the market.

Upper Deck printed these cards and inserted them into their products in the 90s. This was an excellent strategy in both promoting their products and subsequently selling more packs.

These prints contained crash-numbered cards of a limited nature. Some of these cards were autographed, and some of them even came in different colors or an embellishment that made them stand out from the other base cards.

One such rookie card is Mike Trout's 2011 *Topps* Update #US175 Card. Another prime example of a more vintage card is a variation in the print of Mickey Mantle's *Topps* baseball set.

The factor that makes this a one-of-a-kind set is that the numbered sequence between cards #441 and #511 has been printed in both white and yellow lettered cards. Most of his cards have been published in yellow, so getting your hands on a white letter is extremely rare.

The white letters rake up almost seven times as much as their yellow counterparts; however, one has to be mindful of the card's condition, as discussed earlier.

Jerseys and Autographs

Two components influence the price of a sports card when it comes to jersey and autographed cards.

The material used has been discussed earlier and how that contributes to the value of a sports card.

The format in which the autograph was supplied will hold a significant value. When a player has signed a rare card or piece of memorabilia, it will carry more weight than a piece of paper.

If you have a card that holds a patch and has an autograph, you are sitting on a gold mine. Especially if there is a historic event attached to it. For example, Babe Ruth's originally signed Yankee contract has great value.

The value of a signed card can fluctuate as well. This especially rings true for collectors and investors that form part of the pop culture around their sports icons. The value of a signed sports card will remain in high market demand.

A prime example of this case is for athletes such as Babe Ruth, Michael Jordan, Mickey Mantle, and Lou Gehrig.

RANK OF COLORS AND PARALLELS

The 2019-2020 Panini Prizm Basketball Prizms Parallel Gallery

For purposes of using examples, we will delve into all the different types of Panini Prizm cards from the 2019/2020 season.

Base Card
This is the base card of a player, sans any embellishments.

Black Gold Prizms -/5
Where to find them:

- Hobby

Where to buy them:

- eBay

Black Prizms - 1/1
Where to find them:

- Hobby

Where to buy them:

- eBay

Black Shimmer Premium Prizms - 1/1
Where to find them:

- First Off the Line

Where to buy them:

- eBay

Blue Fast Break Prizms - /175
Where to find them:

- Fast Break

Where to buy them:

- eBay

Blue Ice Prizms
Where to find them:

- Hobby

Where to buy them:

- Beckett Marketplace
- eBay

Blue Shimmer Premium Prizms
Where to find them:

- First Off the Line

Where to buy them:

- eBay

Blue Prizms - /199
Where to find them:

- Hobby

Where to buy them:

- Beckett Marketplace
- eBay

Blue, Yellow, and Green Choice Prizms
Where to find them:

- Choice

Where to buy them:

- eBay

Bronze Fast Break Prizms -/20
Where to find them:

- Fast Break

Where to buy them:

- eBay

Fast Break Prizms
Where to find them:

- Fast Break

Where to buy them:

- eBay

Gold Prizms -/10

Where to find them:

- Hobby

Where to buy them:

- eBay

Gold Shimmer Premium Prizms -/10

Where to find them:

- First Off the Line

Where to buy them:

- eBay

Green Choice Prizms -/8

Where to find them:

- Choice

Where to buy them:

- eBay

Green Prizms

Where to find them:

- Blasters
- Gravity Feed
- Multi-Packs
- Retail
- Walmart Hanger Boxes

Where to buy them:

- Beckett Marketplace
- eBay

Green Ice Prizms

Where to find them:

- Fanatics Box

Where to buy them:

- eBay

Green Pulsar Prizms -/25

Where to find them:

- Blasters

Where to buy them:

- Beckett Marketplace
- eBay

Green Shimmer Premium Prizms -/25

Where to find them:

- First Off the Line

Where to buy them:

- eBay

Hyper Prizms

Where to find them:

- Hobby

Where to buy them:

- eBay

Mojo Prizms -/25

Where to find them:

- Hobby

Where to buy them:

- eBay

Nebula Choice Prizms -

Neon Green Fast Break Prizms -/5

Where to find them:

- Fast Break

Where to buy them:

- eBay

Orange Prizms -/49

Where to find them:

- Hobby

Where to buy them:

- eBay

Orange Ice Prizms

Where to find them:

- Walmart Hanger Box

Where to buy them:

- Beckett Marketplace
- eBay

Nebula Choice Prizms - 1/1

Where to find them:

- Choice

Where to buy them:

- eBay

Pink Fast Break Prizms -/50

Where to find them:

- Fast Break

Where to buy them:

- eBay

Pink Ice Prizms

Where to find them:

- Walmart Mega Boxes - you can find up to 10 cards in a box.

Where to buy them:

- Beckett Marketplace
- eBay

Pink Pulsar Prizms -/42

Where to find them:

- Retail

Where to buy them:

- Beckett Marketplace
- eBay

Purple Fast Break Prizms -/75

Where to find them:

- Fast Break

Where to buy them:

- eBay

Purple Pulsar Prizms -/35

Where to find them:

- Gravity Feed

Where to buy them:

- Beckett Marketplace
- eBay

Purple Ice Prizms -/149

Where to find them:

- Hobby

Where to buy them:

- Beckett Marketplace
- eBay

Purple Prizms -/75

Where to find them:

- Hobby

Where to buy them:

- Beckett Marketplace
- eBay

Purple Wave Prizms

Where to find them:

- Blasters

Where to buy them:

- Beckett Marketplace
- eBay

Red Choice Prizms -/88

Where to find them:

- Choice

Where to buy them:

- eBay

Red Ice Prizms

Where to find them:

- Target Mega Box - you can find up to 14 cards in this box.

Where to buy them:

- Beckett Marketplace
- eBay

Red Prizms - /299

Where to find them:

- Hobby

Where to buy them:

- Beckett Marketplace
- eBay

Red Fast Break Prizms -/125

Where to find them:

- Fast Break

Where to buy them:

- eBay

Red, White, and Blue Prizms

Where to find them:

- Multi-Packs - you can find packs with up to three of these cards.

Where to buy them:

- Beckett Marketplace
- eBay

Ruby Wave Prizms

Where to find them:

- Hobby
- Retail

Where to buy them:

- Beckett Marketplace
- eBay

Silver Prizms

Where to find them:

- Blasters
- Choice
- Fanatics Box
- First Off the Line
- Gravity Feed
- Hobby
- Multi-Packs
- Retail
- Target Mega Box

- Walmart Hanger Box
- Walmart Mega Box

Where to buy them:

- Beckett Marketplace
- eBay

Tiger Stripe Choice Prizms
Where to find them:

- Choice

Where to buy them:

- eBay

2020 Panini Prizm Football Base and Parallel Cards

This series is dedicated to all the veterans and vintage greats of the sport. It boasts 300 cards, of which 100 are rookie cards from each NFL franchise.

The parallels are made up of one pair of silver prizms and nine parallels that are numbered per hobby box. The exciting new release of snakeskin prizms produces one card per case.

The green parallels are still exclusive to retail parallels. The various breakdowns are as follows:

China T-Mall Exclusive Parallels

- Base Red & Yellow - #/49
- Rookie Red & Yellow - #/8

Excell Blaster Exclusive Parallels

- Blue

- Disco
- Red

Excell Gravity Feed Exclusive Parallels

- Black & White Checker
- Green

Excell Hanger Box Exclusive Parallels

- Green
- Light Blue

Excell Mega Box Exclusive Parallels

- Pink

Excell Multi-Pack Exclusive Parallels

- Green
- Red, White & Blue

Fanatics Blaster Exclusive Parallels

- Orange Ice

Fanatics Mega Box Exclusive Parallels

- Purple Pulsar

FOTL Exclusive Parallels

- Blue Shimmer - #/25
- Blue Shimmer - #/25
- Red Shimmer - #/35

Hobby Parallels

- Black Finite - 1/1
- Blue Ice - #/99

- Blue Wave - #/199
- Camo - #/25
- Gold - #/10
- Gold Vinyl - #/5
- Green Scope - #/75
- Hyper - #/175
- Orange - #/249
- Purple Power - #/49
- Red Wave - #/149
- Silver
- Snakeskin (one card per case)

MJH Hanger Exclusive Parallels

- Green
- Red Ice

No Huddle Exclusive Parallels

- Blue - #/79
- Neon Green - #/5
- No Huddle Prizm
- Pink - #/15
- Purple - #/35
- Red - #/50

NPP Blaster Exclusive Parallels

- Blue
- Lazer
- Red

NPP Mega Box Exclusive Parallels

- Neon Green Pulsar

NPP Multi-Pack Exclusive Parallels

- Green
- Red, White & Blue

The 2020 Prizm Football Rookie Autograph Parallels Breakdown

Fanatics Mega Box Exclusive Parallels

- Purple Pulsar

FOTL Exclusive Parallels

- Blue Shimmer - #/25
- Green Shimmer - #/5
- Red Shimmer - #/35

Hobby Parallels

- Black Finite - 1/1
- Camo - #/25
- Gold - #/10
- Gold Vinyl - #/5
- Green Scope - #/75 or less
- Purple Power - #/49
- Red Wave - #/149 or less

No Huddle Exclusive Parallels

- Black - 1/1
- Gold - #/10
- No Huddle Prizm

NPP Mega Box Exclusive Parallels

- Black Finite - 1/1
- Gold - #/10

- Neon Green Pulsar
- Prizm - #/99 or less
- Purple Power - #/49 or less

BOX VARIATIONS AND WHERE TO BUY THEM

The majority of sports cards can be found on eBay. Target and Walmart also sell Blasters, Megas, Hangers, and Cellos. All hobby boxes can be bought at any sports cards or hobby shops.

Boxes Sold at Target and Walmart

Some great undiscovered sports card gems can be picked up at Target and Walmart. Some of those boxes contain rare and unique cards that can be sold for up to five times the price you have bought them for.

Such examples include:

NBA *Prizm*

In the retail world, this is the golden arrow of sports card box sets. This includes the mega box sets, hanger boxes, and cello packs. They fetch up to five times more on the market than what you've paid for them in-store.

The NBA RC set is very much in demand this year. So much so that the product retains good value right through. This is due to the inclusion of sporting greats, such as Ja Morant and Zion Williamson.

These are incredibly scarce, but if you get an opportunity, grab onto it with both hands. If you are lucky, you might just find yourself a Ja or a Zion, or even a Silver.

NBA *Optic*

Optic is very similar to *Prizm* and also sells out almost instantly. It does not hold the same worth as *Prizm* but is still very much in demand by collectors and investors alike.

You can get almost double the amount on the open market as what you bought them for.

Recently, a blaster box (averaging $20) sold again for $37. This year's basketball set is just as blessed with up-and-coming sports talent.

The Optic halo range and its color variations are a great find. So, if you see a box, it is definitely worth adding to your collection.

Topps Update

This product, in particular, has seen a sharp spike in sales. This is due to three gents making a big impact in the 2019 season. Gleyber Torres, Juan Soto, and Ronald Acuna Jr are key stakeholders in the sports card collecting hemisphere. Their base rookie cards are worth a lot!

One Shonei Ohtani can also be found in this product, boasting with an RC card and can also rake up quite an amount. The same can be said for athletes such as Shane Beiber, who brings some value as a pitcher to the product. Get this, and you will score big time.

The Calendar Release Dates

During the course of the year, cardboxconnection.com provides critical information on the release dates of each sport and its respective sports cards. This can be viewed when going to their home page.

This is an extremely comprehensive guide from boxes, breakdowns, checklists, and set details. This is then further broken down into the various sports categories. There is a handy search bar that, for example, gives you information on the various sets that are planned for release, as well as when they will be coming out.

— CHAPTER 2 —

TALKING ABOUT SPORTS CARD BRANDS

"I love signing autographs.
I'll sign anything but veal cutlets.
My ballpoint slips on veal cutlets."
—Casey Stengel, Mets, and Yankee skipper.

PREMIUM SPORTS CARD BRANDS

Each sport has its own popular brand that everyone is loyal to and collects or buys the sports cards from.

Trading card manufacturers, a.k.a sports card brands, have been around for many decades. Before unpacking the most well-known sports card brands, you need to do your homework before buying them to see which one is currently dominating the market; this can sometimes be volatile and is ever fluctuating due to factors such as the player's performance and pop culture.

Focus your sights on the below listed popular trading card manufacturers and drown out the lower-end sports card brands' noise.

Topps

Topps started their sports card-producing endeavors in the 20th century. Since then, it has morphed into a multi-million dollar enterprise.

This manufacturer has made sports cards for all four of the major sporting leagues in the U.S.A but has enjoyed popularity for its long stint manufacturing Major League Baseball merchandise.

Its first batch of baseball cards was printed as far back as 1951, but the 1952 set, in particular, saw probably the most sought-after sports card ever being produced—the Mickey Mantle card.

Upper Deck

When this trading card manufacturer made their debut in 1989, they entered the baseball sports card sense with a bang! They caused an unparalleled fever in the sports card collecting field, which had even been experienced before.

Upper Deck became the pioneer of certified autograph cards, game-worn memorabilia cards, and cards with a serial number sequence attached to them.

They are still in the market of manufacturing licensed sets for the National Football League (NFL), and they are the sole sports card manufacturer for the National Hockey League (NHL).

They have also recently announced that they would continue producing baseball cards after a signed deal with the Major League Baseball Players Association (MLBPA).

Upper Deck has brands like SP Authentic and SPx in their arsenal. On these exclusive brands' rosters, sporting legends such as Sidney Crosby and Michael Jordan form part of their spokesmen.

Panini

Panini is a newbie in the field of sports card collecting. The company came to pass in the early 21st century. A lesser-known fact is that it has a parent company known for its production of sports stickers and soccer cards on the European continent.

The Panini Group operates from its headquarters in Modena, Italy. Panini has procured the company World Foot Center. They deal in the promotion and distribution of soccer merchandise for clubs and then for the French national team.

It also has a major share in the Digital Soccer project. This company develops pioneering software in the sports hemisphere.

Bowman

The rich history of *Bowman* sports cards dates back all the way to 1927. You might be surprised to know that in 1930, their main focus was aimed at non-sport-related topics.

In 1939, they introduced their own line of baseball cards. The following three years saw them manufacturing their famous Play Ball sets and catapulted them to sports card stardom.

After World War II, fast forward to 1948 and the rebranding of the company. The *Bowman Gum Company* surfaced as the market leader in the manufacturing of Baseball sports cards.

In 1956, Topps acquired the *Bowman Gum Company* for a mere $200,000. And in 1989, the *Bowman* name was revitalized by *Topps,* and since then, it has been used on some of its subsets of sports cards.

As the Bowman brand grew over the years, *Topps* produced sets such as *Bowman Inception, Bowman Originals, and Bowman Platinum.* These collections aimed to make a top-end feel without compromising the price of the newer premium set, Sterling.

Many of the world's most highly valued and sought-after sports cards were produced, all thanks to *Bowman.* This includes cards such as the 2014 *Bowman* Chrome Prospects Autographed sports card of Kris Bryant and the 2001 *Bowman* Chrome Auto card of Albert Pujols.

Fleer

This company was founded by Frank. H Fleer in 1885 and was the first ever producer of bubble gum.

Their sports card manufacturing journey started in 1923 with the production of baseball cards. They then moved on to make football cards in 1960 and basketball cards in 1986. They even started to produce non-sports trading cards in 1995.

In May 2005, they announced that they would be liquidating the firm. Upper Deck eventually bought them for a cool $6.1 million.

MEDIUM-END SPORTS CARD BRANDS

- Contenders
- Select
- Prizm – mid (most popular on basketball and football) These pretty much control the market.
- Mosaic

LOWER-END SPORTS CARD BRANDS

There are also sports card brands that focus on producing lower-end sports cards. Some of these companies include:

- All-Star
- Crown Royale
- Donruss
- Five Star
- Immaculate
- Leaf
- Oh-Pee-Cee
- Museum
- Play-Off
- Transcendent
- Tribute
- Triple Threads

— CHAPTER 3 —

TYPES OF SPORTS CARD COLLECTIONS

"Signing autographs was fun until a kid came up to me and said, "My dad says you're getting old, you're going to die, and your autograph will be valuable." - Warren Spahn, HOF pitcher who played until he was 44.

A sports card collector or investor can employ many tactics to grow their portfolio. Below are our top ten pro tips for managing and expanding your collection, and accomplishing your individual goal:

1. Choose a collection theme, and stick to it as much as possible before branching out.
2. Purchase graded or authenticated sports cards.
3. Ask the right questions and do your due diligence before buying anything. This can be achieved by buying our guide to *7 things you must do before buying a sports card.*

4. Ensure that you only buy sports cards from reputable brands and sellers on online platforms and in hobby stores.
5. Before your collection grows, consider where you will be storing or displaying your portfolio. Be mindful of elements, such as the sun, that might impact your card's quality and degrade its value.
6. Don't become a bargain hunter, and always investigate the current market value to offer a fair price to a seller. They might just be open to negotiating; there is no harm in asking.
7. Purchase the best quality for your budget.
8. Keep calm, keep your emotions intact, but don't be afraid to go and get what you are after. It is a delicate balance!
9. Remember that an expert opinion always trumps provenance any day.
10. Have fun, always. If it is not fun anymore, this is not the hobby for you. Passion is key.

THE DIFFERENT TYPES OF SPORTS CARDS COLLECTIONS ON OFFER

Set Building

A set collector is an individual who builds their collection using specific sets from every product instead of collecting an individual team or a particular player.

In essence, set building is putting back in order what has been disarranged. It is imperative that you do your homework before engaging in set building or deciding on this as a course of action towards growing your portfolio.

Sure, you need to have knowledge of the rookies and the other stars and their cards. But you should also look out for a higher-numbered series that might be scarce. You can then put further research into to enquire if there are short-printed cards available.

At first, you might not have the heart to fork out more money for a 2014 *Topps* Heritage short print (they are very common), as you might pay less for a genuine 1956 sports card of the same bracket.

There is also the risk of purchasing error cards and different variations, so you need to consider this before getting pulled in. Base sets and master sets are not newcomers to the hobby.

In fact, the 1956 set of *Topps* has six team cards, with three different variations.

The different types of sets can be categorized as follows:

Base Sets or Regular Sets

Base cards and regular sets form the basics of each trading card set. They are the most common type of cards you can find in a pack and are also called "commons" sometimes.

Each regular card will have a number on the back, making it form part of a complete set.

Insert Sets

These are sets that are planned short prints. They are extremely popular, and collectors are very excited about them. These cards' ratios found in any insert pack can be only one card per pack or a 1:1 ratio. This means that there is only one card of this type in existence.

Multiple Series Sets

In any given year, card manufacturers will craft multiple series' cards to capture all of the rookies from that sport and the most highest traded players in the entire set.

Some collectors and investors are loyal to a brand, decide on a few brands per annum, and then focus on building a complete set. These sport card enthusiasts want a card of the latest rookie to the team, or they would like to see a card with their favorite athlete sporting a different type of kit.

For this reason, manufacturers such as Upper Deck Baseball have a two-parter series. The first half is released to the public early in the year, and the second series is released in the middle of the season.

In some cases, an update set is released at the end of the season to capture some of the year's highlights.

Parallel Sets

A parallel set refers to a point in time when the general layout of a card is repurposed. The parallel group will look identical to the regular set but in a more enhanced way.

Parallel sets are manufactured with different paper, different tech, extra foils, and anything that can be done to embellish the card differently, giving it a more decadent feel.

Subsets

Subsets are designed to give you the chance to see your favorite athletes on different designs and themes from any one set. This is a great option if you are seeking more variety in your card collection. These types of sports cards are the most commonly found type in packs.

Player Collection

A Player Collector is an individual who picks particular players and builds a set based on those cards. The art of collecting players has its advantages and disadvantages.

Player collections can be classified as collecting cards of only one player, and other collectors might be in hot pursuit of a few players. Some collectors go as specific as collecting cards from a player within a particular team, as opposed to collecting cards for one single player throughout their career with different teams.

This is a very popular form of sports card collecting. There is no prescribed best practice way of going about this, but even casual collectors are known to keep a secret stash on the side of their favorite athlete/athletes.

A big drawing card of this type of collection is that you will find affordable cards. Except for vintage cards, where the athlete you are seeking might only have a few cards. But, if it's a well-known player, there is undoubtedly a plethora of cheap cards to collect, especially outside the era before World War II started.

You might even be lucky enough to find sports cards from the 70s and 80s. Most cards that were produced after the war can be affordable. However, you would need to compromise on the state of them. You can find real gems for under $1. That's the easy part!

If you are a die-hard fan who literally wants all the cards of your particular hero, well strap yourself in, as this is where the ride gets bumpy.

As you can imagine, these cards might be pricey. Suppose that you find some of these cards. You might be surprised to know that they aren't that expensive, but you will have to perform a deep-dive session to locate them.

For example, some athletes from the 80s and 90s have scarce cards, and finding them is like looking for a needle in a haystack.

Team Collection

This is a collector that has a niche of collecting teams for their portfolio. This is also sometimes referred to as a team set.

The concept of team set building is a notion as old as sports card collecting itself. This is one of the most popular forms of sports card collecting. The idea of collecting separate cards to build an entire team set is not as common as it used to be.

This is because the sports card manufacturers identified the value of stardom and fandom early on.

More so, collectors were not interested in collecting cards of a bunch of random players. Instead, they prefer to trade sports cards from their local teams. Collectors and investors still adopt the concept of trading sports cards from teams in their local area or city, today.

The most popular team sets to be collected were printed in the 30s. The 1935 Detroit Free Press set (M120) contained a collection of images published by the newspaper of the same name. The set consisted of team images such as the Detroit Tigers.

In 1930 and 1931, respectively, a beverage company called Ribbon Malt published images of the White Sox and the Chicago Cubs. Other sports card manufacturers made team sets that were photographed. One such set was the 1938 Sawyer Biscuit set. These cards were printed inside a red frame made from cardboard.

Parallel Rainbow Collection

A Rainbow Parallel card collection refers to the complete range of all the possible parallel colors of one particular player's specific card. In the words of author Mark Twain, "One can enjoy a rainbow without necessarily forgetting the forces that made it."

A complete set of rainbow parallels is an achievement with promising bragging rights of note. This is the ultimate show of adoration for a team or a player in the sports card hemisphere and a sign of commitment and dedication.

The amount of input will depend on the rainbow's size and how hard you will have to work to achieve your goal. It is the perfect storm of pieces that must all join together like a puzzle!

For example, rainbow parallel cards from the 2017 *Topps* range are categorized by the distinctively different surfaces. Some variations, such as the Clear and the Rainbow Foil cards, each bear its own distinctive face.

The images appear to resemble melted metal from a negative perspective and are easy to spot. However, the color-based sports cards might need another look. They are spotted by the prevalence of two triangles in a pennant-shape on the top part of the card and are located just beneath the name tag.

Alternatively, other means include checking for a serial number. However, the serial number can be minimal in some instances, and you might miss them if you quickly scan through a pack of cards.

It may be overwhelming to you in that it might seem like there are many parallels in existence, but there might be only 50 copies or fewer that were produced. *Topps*' gallery of rainbow parallels are categorized as follows:

- 65th Anniversary card

- Base card
- Black card
- Clear card
- Father's Day card in powdered blue
- Gold card
- The Memorial Day card in camo
- Mother's day card in hot pink
- Negative black and white card
- Platinum card
- The printing plates card in black
- The printing plates card in cyan blue
- The printing plate card in magenta
- The printing plates card in yellow
- Purple card
- Rainbow foil card
- Vintage stock card

Vintage Collection

Collectors and investors agree that vintage sports cards are classified as those that were manufactured before 1980. The jury is not conclusively out as yet, as some feel that anything produced in the 70s and 60s does not count as vintage.

For anything to be classified as vintage, it needs to be at least 20 years old and must hold some form of importance. There is another term that is also used, and that is called the junk era sports cards.

These cards are given this name due to having originated in the mass-producing era between 1980 to the mid-1990s.

— CHAPTER 4 —

THE IMPORTANCE OF GRADING CARDS

"Always give an autograph when somebody asks you. You never can tell. In baseball, anything can happen." —Tommy Lasorda. He gave this piece of advice to Dodgers rookies annually during spring training.

Naturally, there are many different opinions based on whether or not you should get your sports cards graded. Since most collectors and investors trade online, in our opinion, this is very important.

However, some avid sports card enthusiasts feel that, if a card from a mass-produced range is graded, it is almost never worth the paper it has been printed on. In essence, their opinion means that they feel you will pay more to have the card graded than what it is actually worth.

Sure, there are exceptions to the rule. But generally speaking, it is not recommended to have a card graded from the 1990

Fleer or *Donruss* baseball card collections. These are two of the most over-manufactured sets in sports card history.

The only two brands that we recommend for you to pay to have your cards graded. These are:

- *Professional Sports Authenticator (PSA)*
- *Beckett Grading System (BGS)*

They are the foremost leaders in sports card grading services. To be honest, their services don't come cheap, but you will have peace of mind that when you decide to sell your graded cards, they will be bought due to the PSA and BGS seals of approval.

OUR PRO-TIP ADVICE FOR GRADING SPORTS CARDS

Your rookie card collection is the best to send for grading. Sports card enthusiasts will pay top dollar for high-graded rookie cards from the best athletes of the most scarcest sets produced.

You might want to consider having your Chase cards and sets graded. But you need to do your homework first to check that these cards did not originate from mass-produced sets and also check that the athlete is currently performing, as this might influence the price of the card when you resell it.

Both the BGS and PSA have websites where you are able to see how many cards have been graded of the ones you are considering getting graded. As an added bonus, both of the graders' web pages provide you with a pop report (population report) that gives you the data of how many cards were graded per set.

This works by looking up a card. Let's use the 1952 Mickey Mantle RC #311 as an example. You will be given access to the data to show how many PSA 10 cards have been graded for this card. Similarly, you can also look at other Mantle RC cards.

Newer sets have a tendency to produce a high pop rate.

Again, this might be completely overwhelming in the beginning. But, think of it this way, it is not a clear-cut decision and is influenced by many different factors. However, with lots of research and practice, you will come to know which cards are worth getting graded and which aren't.

THE BENEFITS OF SPORTS CARD GRADING

The two major sports card authentication companies can offer a range of benefits. *PSA*, in particular, can provide the following benefits to those that make use of their grading services:

Established registry
PSA has formulated a unique registry that provides limitless possibilities in terms of card collecting and makes it fun for all parties concerned.

Established price guide
SMR has developed a set price guide where investors and collectors alike enjoy increased market stability.

Increased value
PSA aids the sellers to get the full worth of their cards when reselling due to the PSA seal of authentication.

Information at your fingertips
PSA Cardfacts® provides critical data on the player, the card origins, and other valuable information.

Protection
PSA places each graded card into a sealed tamper-proof case. These plastic pockets provide protection against the elements, and you can be confident that they are well-protected and won't damage.

Set standards
PSA possesses universally recognized standards and is respected worldwide for its expertise.

SENDING CARDS FOR GRADING

Grading Submission Types

When sending cards for grading, there are four different types of submissions to choose from:

Crossover
This option is ideal for you if you want to have your cards regraded from a previous authenticator to another company, for example, from *SGC* to *PSA*.

Grading
This process refers to the authentication and grading of a raw card (a card that has not been graded previously). The *BGS* or *PSA* will then award it with an appropriate grade from their scaling systems.

Reholder

This option is used when you wish to reseal a card previously graded by the same authenticator, and you want to place it in the most recent capsule of the grading company.

Review

You will select this option, almost as an appeal. So you might feel that a previously graded card might be worth more, and then you will re-submit the card to the grader.

HOW TO PREPARE A CARD FOR GRADING

Get your biggest ROI on cards by performing this quick recipe on preparing your cards for the grading process.

Items required

- A cheap game-used card
- Card savers
- Graded card bags
- Microfiber cloths
- Magnifier with a light
- Printing paper
- Penny sleeves
- Rubber gloves

Directions

1. Put on the rubber gloves before doing anything.
2. Remove the card from its current penny sleeve. Also, remove the top loader, if applicable.

3. Scrutinize the card through the magnifying glass. Check the corners in both the front and the back of the card.
4. Check the surface for damage such as scratches, discolorations, etc. Again apply this process on both the back as well as the front of the card.
5. Place the sports card face down on a clean, white sheet of printing or photocopy paper.
6. Using the microfiber cloth, wipe both sides of the card. **It is imperative that you only clean in one direction of the card.**
7. Using the photocopy paper, flip the card over to the other side. Repeat the wiping process.
8. Use the magnifying glass to inspect the whole card on all sides to ensure that you have cleaned off any pollutants, dirt, and fingerprints from the card.
9. Once you are satisfied that the card has been thoroughly cleaned, place it into a new penny sleeve. Place the card down on the photocopy paper.
10. Take the dummy card and place it inside the card saver. Push it in and take it out a few times and push the sides out. This will open the card saver up to receive the card in its penny sleeve.
11. Insert the card in the penny sleeve into the card saver. You will find that it will easily slot into the card saver pocket.
12. Next, place the card saver into the graded card sleeve bag and seal it with the sticky side.

Pro tips for prepping

- Never reuse the penny sleeve that you received the card in, no matter how long it was inside the sleeve.

It would not make sense to reinsert a freshly cleaned card into a used sleeve that contains dust particles and other pollutants.

- Take extra care with chrome sports cards as they require a more intense cleaning process. If necessary, repeat the cleaning process a few times.
- The best possible advice we have is for you to be a much harsher critic than you would expect from the authenticators before submitting a sports card for appraisal.
- Most of the items you will need can be purchased from Amazon.

SUBMITTING YOUR CARD FOR GRADING

For this particular section, we will describe *PSA's* process for submission.

1. After completing the preparation phase, organize your cards by making separate piles of the same category or sport.
2. Next, take those piles and organize them by year.
3. After you have organized them by year, split the packs into players or the insert of that set and the year.
4. Create your account on the *PSA* website.
5. Choose the item type that you will be submitting.
6. Select your submission type.
7. Choose your service level.
8. Enter the descriptions of your cards in the appropriate fields.

9. Using a box, place some bubble wrap or air pillows at the bottom of the box.
10. Wrap your cards in rubber bands.
11. Place more padding such as bubble wrap or air pillows on the top of the cards.
12. Pick the box up and shake it. If the contents are moving around, you need to add additional padding until it remains firmly in place.
13. Add your submission paper on the very top.
14. Seal the box and ship.

Pro tips for shipping

- Never use scotch tape or shipping tape to wrap your cards in. *PSA* has a preference for rubber bands.
- If you send batches of cards for grading, don't wrap more than 50 cards in a pile with a rubber band.

TABLES

State of Cards PSA

#	Abbreviation	Meaning
1.	*PR 1*	Poor
2.	*FR 1.5*	Fair
3.	*Good 2*	Good
4.	*VG 3*	Very Good
5.	*VG-EX 4*	Very Good-Excellent
6.	*EX 5*	Excellent
7.	*EX-MT 6*	Excellent-Mint

8.	*NM 7*	Near Mint
9.	*NM-MT 8*	Near Mint-Mint
10.	*Mint 9*	Mint
11.	*GEM-MT 10*	Gem-Mint

State of Cards Beckett

#	Abbreviation	Meaning
1.	*1*	Poor
2.	*1.5*	Fair
3.	*2 G*	Good
4.	*2.5*	G+
5.	*3 VG*	Very Good
6.	*3.5*	VG+
7.	*4 VG-EX*	Very Good-Excellent
8.	*4.5*	VG-EX+
9.	*5 EX*	Excellent
10.	*5.5*	EX+
11.	*6 EX-NM*	Excellent-Near Mint
12.	*6.5*	EX-NM+
13.	*7*	Near Mint
14.	*7.5*	Near Mint+
15.	*8*	Near Mint-Mint
16.	*9*	Mint
17.	*9.5*	Gem Mint
18.	*10*	Pristine

WHY PSA IS THE PREFERRED SPORTS CARD AUTHENTICATOR

We live in strange times, a.k.a., the Covid era. Unfortunately, each and every person and business sector on this planet has been impacted by Covid somehow. Naturally, this has also extended to the sports card collecting hemisphere.

At the time of writing this book, the *PSA* operations have not been restored in full due to tough lockdown and trading restrictions in the country. This has resulted in a severe backlog that has seen *PSA* have to develop innovative ways of dealing with the current backlog and growing backlog.

Their "bulk submissions" feature has now been rebranded as a "value submissions" feature. Their current turnaround times (at the time of writing this book) for submissions are as follows:

- *Reholder* - 60 business days.
- *Dual submission* (regular service) - 100+ business days.
- *Card submission* (regular service) - 73 business days.
- *Ticket submission* (regular/economy service) - 72 business days.
- *Card submission* (bulk service) - 100+ business days.

There is no denying that these pictures depict a bleak outlook with a long waiting time. Even with the current lag experienced, no other sports card authenticator comes close to *PSA* when it comes to ROI!

With the *SCG* rating system, sports card collectors experienced that not only did the cards battle to sell that had the *SCG* approval stamp on, but they did not nearly sell as much, which means the collectors and investors had to input a lot of manual labor into flipping the cards after a long time on the market.

Collectors and investors have reported losses ranging between 25%–50%. Nevermind the losses! But don't take our word for it. Go and inspect both websites for the number of cards sold for any card you desire and let the results speak for themselves.

You might even be surprised that the myth of SGC being better for vintage cards is dispelled based on this very premise? Think about it this way—isn't the prestige of your personal cards, awaiting appraisal worth waiting three to six months for, and then receiving a high ROI---**every single time**?

Ask yourself these questions:

- How many SGC graded cards have you bought?
- Have those cards increased in value?
- What was the return on investment for you?

— CHAPTER 5 —

BUYING AND SELLING SPORTS CARDS

"I felt like my bubble gum card collection had come to life." —Actor James Garner.

SECRET CRITERIA OF BUYING SPORTS CARDS

There is a secret list of methodologies that we like to use and that we are more than happy to share with you. Take all of these factors into consideration before purchasing a sports card:

Graded vs. raw cards

If you are thinking about collecting or investing in raw sports cards, you might want to take some time to understand all of the intricacies around it. For someone just starting out, it might be hard to grade using the naked eye.

However, some are of the opinion that raw cards should be graded, as this adds to the level of authenticity needed to be able to make a good return on investment once it has been resold.

Factoring in that both buying and selling raw can provide a lucrative outcome.

The sports card authenticator

As discussed in a previous chapter, PSA and Beckett are top of the log when it comes to sports card grading. They are reputable and respected grading houses. When checking any sales platform, you will immediately note that cards that they have graded sell for more than those graded by other brands.

The rise of alternative brands

Other brands, like *Nike,* have started to produce their own sets of sports cards. Currently, *Panini* dominates football and basketball rankings, and *Topps* has the driving seat for baseball cards.

Bear in mind that this is a volatile market, and the landscape might change in a few years. So it might not hurt getting some of these cards in the meantime.

The rank of the player

The rank and the performance of the player on the field are both significant deciding factors when it comes to the selection criteria. We recommend looking at ESPN's rankings per sport for the most up-to-date information on rankings for the various sports types.

The player's talent

You might find the idea of taking a gamble on who the next top rookie will be over the next few years and then invest in some of their rookie cards. Most collectors use the player's name as the departure point and then branch it out to factors such as:

- Draft class based on the pop report.
- The aesthetic value of the card.
- The entry price.
- The current price when compared to the stars on the sports star's draft that is found on the draft class of the athlete.

The player's off-field conduct

The manner in which an athlete conducts themselves outside of the sport also impacts the card's value.

Naturally, if they partake in philanthropy endeavors, this will make them more valuable. However, if they do anything controversial in terms of pop culture or otherwise, this will negatively impact their card's value.

The same can be said that some sports icons' cards are still valuable, even though they might be diseased or long-retired from the game.

The player's team

Take the major markets into consideration when it comes to the team's overall performance. The team might not be having a good season, but the player might be extremely popular, and vice versa.

HOW TO CHECK THE PRICES ON SPORTS CARDS

Checking Card Prices on eBay - a Step-by-Step Guide

1. In the search field box, type the title name of the card or any related keywords of the item that you wish to find.
2. Click on the search box feature.
3. You will be taken to the search results page.
4. Select the Sold Listings checkbox to see items that have sold (and how much they have sold for previously) as far back as the eBay search engine will permit. (currently, you can go and look for products sold as far back as three months.
   - If you are on a desktop, go to the left-hand sidebar and scroll down to the Show Only option under that menu. Make sure you check the Sold Items and Completed Items.
   - If you are on your cell phone, tap on, then scroll down and select the Sold Items and Completed Items.
5. Once eBay has provided the sold listings, select the preferred sorting method.
6. You will be presented with a dropdown box menu, providing the following options:
   - *End Date: Recent First:* Provides a list for the most recently sold items first.
   - *Date Listed: Oldest First:* Displays items that were sold from the oldest listings to the newest.
   - *Distance: Nearest First:* This sort only helps if you are looking for items sold close to you; otherwise,

it might not be of much benefit in this instance. You are looking for pricing information.

- *Price+ Shipping: Lowest First:* Provides a listicle of items from the lowest price attained to the highest price paid per article.
- *Price+ Shipping:* Highest First: Lists the completed items from highest to lowest.

Pro tips for checking card prices on eBay:

1. If the number is green, this implies that the price it sold for is scratched, which means that the seller was made a lower offer and accepted this.
2. Look for scratched prices on eBay using this link: https://130point.com.
3. When you see scratched-off prices on it, it implies the seller accepted an offer, and the scratched price is not the number they agree on. To look up the actual amount the seller received, check out this website: https://130point.com/sales/
4. Always check the price on a card before making any type of purchase.

A Step-by-Step Guide for Checking Card Prices on PWCC

Research historic auction and sale prices (this feature is more commonly used in the instance of older cards). www.pwccmarketplace.com has a service where you can find sale data dating as far back as 15 years.

You are able to search the sales history of a sports card from 2004. This is a complimentary service to the public in joint efforts to entice the public to participate in marketplace sports card trading. To date, this sports card sales database has a retrospective report structure of over 200 million transactions.

This makes it the world's largest singular set of data pertaining to sales. As a side note, it is important to note that the information is mostly unfiltered and raw, and additional research may be required. The edited information is categorized as:

- The availability of images is only given for sales after March 2018.
- Any listing that contains the word "reprint" is not included in the search results.
- The Sold Price filter defaults to $50 but can be decreased to $0 if needs be.
- The Sale Type filter defaults to "auction sales only." And can include fixed-price sales if needs be.
- Items that fall under the "unpaid" category are removed from the database, representing no true marketplace value.

The instructions

1. Navigate to the website.
2. In the top white search bar, enter the year and the name of the card manufacturer, and the player's name.
3. Scroll down to the "Time frame" bar and select the appropriate year/s you wish to see the sales for.
4. Proceed to the "Sold Price Range" bar on the right and select the appropriate data.
5. This will produce an arrangement of search results.
6. The information can then be sorted into:
    - *Sort: Date: Newest First*

- *Sort: Date: Oldest First*
- *Price: Highest First*
- *Price: Lowest First*
- *Auction Price Only*
- *Fixed Price Only*
- *Auction & Fixed Price*

SPORTS CARD TRADING AND NEGOTIATION

Throughout this book, a recurring theme is not to be afraid to put your negotiating skills to the test or develop the skill as you trade cards on various online marketplaces.

When you see that the sports card that you want is listed in the budget range that you are willing to spend on it, and providing that it is in the *Buy It Now* (BIN) category on eBay, you can try to offer the seller a lower price than advertised, but make sure that it is a fair offer.

When making a purchase on any other platforms, such as Facebook and Marketplace, the same can be said—always try to negotiate with the seller as far as possible and see if they are open to the notion.

The Buy It Now Feature on eBay

The aim here is to turn the offer in your favor. You can save quite a bit of your money with this feature on the eBay platform. It allows any potential buyer to bypass the bidding cycle to close the auction sooner at a consented price between the two stakeholders.

You might just be lucky enough that the seller actually accepts your counteroffer.

There is a determining factor at play that will dictate the deal's outcome to sway it in your favor. This is entirely dependent on the offer that the seller agrees to when the offer is made.

The *Buy It Now* feature will stay on the auction page until the first bid has been placed and will then disappear. The only exception to this rule is in the case of reserve-price auctions, where the feature will be enabled until the reserve has been fulfilled, no matter the number of bids received. This tidbit of information can be played to your advantage.

Using BIN to your advantage

Some of the best deals are listed under the BIN category. The seller will indicate a meager BIN price, which allows you to grab this first as the winning bidder. If you feel the offer is reasonable and have the disposable income to buy it, then go for it!

All that you need to do is to scroll to the BIN tab in the search results and organize the listings by *Newly Listed*. The BIN auctions will be ranked on top of this list. This will provide you with an excellent opportunity to cash in on the early deals, as they tend to disappear after a few hours, if not sooner. <u>**Pro-Tip: There may be a valid reason that an auction has a low Buy It Now price; be sure to read the product description carefully before you commit to a purchase. And be mindful of fraudsters who force buyers to obligate themselves for the completion of Buy It Now transactions instead of those that conclude normally.**</u>

The Current eBay Fee Structure

Every time a seller lists on eBay, they are charged a certain type of selling fee. The two main types of selling fees are:

1. **Insertion fees** - when a seller creates a listing.
2. **Final value fees** - when an item is sold.

Insertion fees explained

Every month, a seller is given a total of 200 zero insertion fee listings. This will be more if they have an actual eBay e-commerce store associated with their profile. When their zero insertion fee listings have been used, the following insertion fees will apply:

- Non-refundable if their item hasn't sold.
- They are charged per listing and per category. So, if their item is listed in two different categories, they will pay an insertion fee for each category.
- They are charged for the initial listing, and each time an item is relisted.
- Sellers are charged per listing if they create duplicate auction-style listings for the same items.

Final value fees explained

eBay charges a final value fee when a seller's item has been sold.

This fee is calculated as a percentage of the total amount of the sale. The sale's total amount refers to the amount the buyer pays, including applicable shipping and handling costs.

RECENT UPDATES FROM EBAY

In 2020, eBay announced that they would be making updates to their processes by adding a new shipping tracking service called eBay Standard Envelope. They will also be updating their Return Policy.

This is an exclusive product for trading card sellers. It allows the sports card trading collectors a cost-effective way of selling and shipping sports cards at virtually the exact cost of a postage stamp.

Sellers will now benefit from selling lower-priced cards without paying a premium price for it when it is shipped to the buyer.

The tracking service associated with the latest product is at the advantage of both the seller and the buyer. The seller is protected, and their product shipping becomes more affordable in the process without having to pay USPS first-class rates.

Lastly, the seller will receive the top-tiered benefits associated with the new service.

eBay Standard Envelope

EBay's new service offering permits sports card collecting enthusiasts an affordable way of shipping their highly valued trading cards for a value up to $20. It is a seamless and straightforward way to send trading cards with complete peace of mind and offers integrated tracking solutions.

Some of its features include:

That it is easy to use
You only need to print your label and send it via USPS.

Secure shipping solutions

You can save up to 70% with the budget-friendly shipping options that have integrated tracking solutions associated with them.

Additional benefits

The individual that makes use of the shipping service has benefits attached, such as qualifying and maintaining a top-tiered status and ensuring that every shipment is insured and protected. You will receive the badge, the search benefits attached to your listing, as well as a 10% discount on the value of the sale.

Previously, in terms of protection, the seller had to choose whether or not to use an inexpensive shipping method at the risk of not being protected.

How to use eBay's new Standard Envelope service

You can start using eBay's new feature in as little as three steps from both a selling and a buying perspective.

Selling

1. **List your sports trading cards.** Create a listing for one or more cards on your eBay seller's profile under the standard shipping envelope section as a shipping method.
2. **Shipping the cards you sold.** Print the relevant labels from eBay labels, attach them to the package, and then send it via the United States Postal Service. The tracking solution is automatically integrated into the package.
3. **Tracking your shipment.** You are then able to track the relevant progress via the *Seller Hub* or *My eBay* tabs.

Buying

1. **Find the card/s that you want to buy.** Select a card with a value of up to $20, whereby the eBay Standard Envelope forms part of the tracking service.
2. **Tracking the card after your purchase.** You can monitor the process of your shipment by reviewing your *My eBay Purchase* tab.
3. **Receiving your parcel.** This is the last step in the process for you as a buyer. This is when your parcel is safely and securely in your hands.

You can start shipping any time from today for the following weight and price structures:

- 1oz - $o.51
- 2oz - $o.71
- 3oz - $0.91

eBay Disclaimers:

This is subject to weight and dimensional requirements as specified on the website.

This service is not available for graded cards and only in the instance of raw sports trading cards.

The service is open to sports cards, non-sports cards, and collectible cards only with a value of $20 and less.

Updated Return Policy

eBay has become a pioneer in e-commerce trading, in that almost any item thinkable can be purchased from the site. So much so that eBay's GM of Trading Cards and Collectibles, Nicole Colombo, announced in an interview with Sportscardinvestor.

com that she has personally spent a lot of time investigating the needs of the sports card trading community.

She found that many service offerings from eBay are not at all suited to sports cards and other collectors' requirements—so much so that she felt the need to request that eBay's return policy in terms of sports card traders be revised and amended for them to gain some benefit from it.

Before this amendment, the seller had the option to choose which options they want to present to the seller in terms of returns. However, to have access to these benefits, the sellers were forced to choose the 30-day return option.

Very few people in the sports card trading community are aware that sellers only have to choose 14-days for returns. However, eBay felt that this is still a very long window for sellers of sports cards.

Subsequently, they decided to also review the "remorse return window" as of January 2021. The seller can now choose their return policy for the number of days suited to their preference and still qualify for eBay's top-tiered benefits.

The eBay money-back guarantee

In the same interview, Nicole Colombo also announced that they are looking into changing the eBay money-back guarantee. There is no further information available at this time, but worth mentioning for future purposes.

Managed payments for sellers

Another recent change from eBay saw one of the most significant changes being made to the platform recently. From an overall management perspective, this is a beneficial feature to both buyers and sellers.

It works on eBay's premises of now managing your payments, and it won't be facilitated via PayPal any longer. Going forward, PayPal will still be a payment option that eBay accepts, but there will be a plethora of other payment options available.

Some of these include:

- Apple Pay
- Credit card payments
- Debit card payments
- Google Pay

The added benefit for sellers is that instead of paying two sets of fees (eBay fees and PayPal fees), they will only have to pay eBay fees, thus saving them even more money.

This feature is already available to some sellers, and other sellers will benefit from it during the 2021 financial year.

eBay is very much focused on making the lives of sports card traders easier by allowing them to take charge of all the available features on their platform and having eBay facilitate this on their behalf. Some of these features when making use of consignors are:

1. Creating the sports card listings as a proxy party.
2. Managing the complete end-to-end process.
3. They will make the call on deciding which method would be the best to sell the cards (Best offer, Auction, etc.)
4. Managing the entire customer service process.
5. Getting involved in the shipment cycle.

The seller only needs to decide to go directly onto eBay to facilitate the process themselves or make use of the consignors such as PWCC or Outstanding123. Choosing to engage on this level with these two well-known consignors will ensure an increase in seller value.

It should be mentioned that consignors also charge fees, which needs to be considered. This especially rings true for those sports cards a seller would want to sell on an auction on eBay.

eBay tips for selling directly onto the platform

- Ensure that every listing has keywords in the title related to the sports card you are selling.
- Take a few high-quality images of your sports cards that you are planning to sell. This will ensure that they are sold faster, especially in the case of raw cards.
- Don't use a stock image of the card that you are selling, but an actual photograph.
- Ensure that the card's front and back are shown, with all of the details clearly visible that a prospective buyer would want to see when purchasing a card.
- Be open to buyer communication.
- List as much detail about your card as possible.
- Chat to buyers and answer their questions on the messaging option.
- Ensure that the relevant shipping details are listed and in an easy spot to find on your listing, as the buyer will consider this before making a purchase.
- Provide a tracking option to buyers.

- Make use of the new eBay standard envelope service as much as possible.
- Attend eBay's seller school to educate yourself and to ensure that you get as much as possible out of every listing.

eBay tips for sports card buyers

- Follow all of the sellers that you are considering buying sports cards from. This way, you will receive push notifications advising you of any new listings created by them and any changes in their sports cards' pricing.
- Save all of your searches for sports cards.
- Make use of all of the buyer features associated with the listing.

CHECKING FOR EBAY COMPS

eBay is a valuable tool for studying the sales history on the card when it comes to historical information, such as all the completed sales and listings sold over a certain period of time.

This is an essential feature for both buyers and sellers to indicate how much you should list a card for and how much you can expect to pay for it.

It is a simple process that involves typing in the card's name and selecting the time period of retrospective sales that you want to view. You can use this feature to check cards one by one.

It is vital that this "test" is conducted every time before you create a listing or purchase a new card due to the volatility of the market. The entire arena can change with only the sale of one card.

This rings especially true when amid a bidding war and knowing when to hold or when to fold, depending on your budget and how badly you want to add that card to your portfolio or collection.

Another important red flag to look out for is in the instance of trying to avoid shill bidders. A shill bidder is an individual who probably already owns a particular card. They then open up a new eBay account and escalate the card's price via the auction method, or Buy Now, but they never have the intention of actually paying that seller.

Many sports card collectors and traders are faced with this occurrence in the hobby. It will only take one such bad experience to put anyone off from engaging in such activity again.

Another deep-diving session into the comp analysis will be required to try and mitigate the situation. For example:

1. Click on the *Auction* button located at the top of the page after selecting sold and completed items. This way, you can have an overview of sports cards sold via auction and then review the bids received on that particular item.
2. A page will then open where you can review all of the buyers who bid on the card in that particular auction. You will clearly see the page of buyers that do not have any form of feedback attached to their profile they entered the bid from.
3. Be careful in automatically assuming that this is a fake account. Every day many new sports card traders create an eBay profile in an attempt to purchase sports cards. Typically, their bids will be $10 higher than the last bid entered.

4. Another method of checking is to go and look at the detailed bidding history of a particular bidder. However, this still won't be a clear indication of whether you are dealing with a fraudster or not. And it will also create an impossible loop of knowing for sure what the card's value is.

Another way to check might be to review the item again to see if the seller has relisted it. But bear in mind that a seller might only receive payment a week or more after the sale has been completed, and there might be a myriad of legitimate reasons for it.

A con artist wants to buy the card at a higher price than its market value to inflate its worth. When they don't pay the seller, the seller is then forced to relist the item again.

To ensure that you are paying what is called fair market price, do the following:

- Check out the multiple listings on eBay for the same card.
- Review the auction history and pay attention to buyers that have no feedback (shill bidders).
- Review the history of bidders to see if they have placed bids on more than one auction.
- Check if the item had to be relisted.
- Take to the support team of eBay for assistance.

Also, don't be afraid to reach out to other platforms, such as Facebook and Discord, and your fellow sports card traders for guidance and advice.

EBAY LISTINGS

Red Flags to Look out for When It Comes to Scamming

There are many con artists online, and unfortunately, it is no different when it comes to sports card trading. They will always try to think a few steps ahead of an ethical person to try and play on your emotions.

Some tips for spotting these fraudsters are:

Checking whether they have any feedback from sellers

Fraudsters are incredibly creative in even going as far as fabricating positive feedback. They cleverly buy some low-hanging fruit and then make fraudulent listings in an attempt to sell those items.

These articles are sometimes purchased at prices starting with $0.01, and they buy these items from big sellers on eBay.

In turn, the big sellers employ the services of an array of software apps that have been programmed to create this so-called feedback. This is significant to the seller's advantage as they can receive input quickly for a low price to pay.

Pay careful attention to a seller that has many positive ratings and feedback that has happened over a few days in succession. Also, be wary when they have listed a completely random bunch of items that have no relation to each other at all.

Again, this seller might not be a fraudster but do your homework thoroughly before engaging with them.

The $500 sales gimmick

An unethical seller will try to sell their cards around the $500 mark or create a bunch of listings that surmounts to $500. The reason for this is that PayPal has a cap on monthly withdrawal transactions totaling $500 or more for account holders that have not confirmed their accounts.

A con artist is, in fact, very lazy and wants to make the minimum amount of effort, so verifying a Paypal account is not even considered. PayPal requires credit and bank-related info before confirming an account. The fraudsters won't do this, as they will then run the risk of a paper trail.

In the instance of sports cards, the scammer will then, for example, list a few sports cards for a reduced amount, such as $50 per card, and then will put the listing up as a sale for that particular day only. Check out the sports card listings they have created and their other items for sale under eagle eye review.

Bear in mind that one item totaling $500 is not a clear indication that this is an illegitimate transaction but rather a red flag that requires further scrutiny.

If it does not feel right

Trust your gut. It is said that if something feels too good to be true, 99% of the time, it is too good to be true! Any person who has gone through the trouble of creating their eBay profile, setting up their banking and financial profiles, and creating a listing has definitely done their due diligence on the amount that the sports card is worth before selling it.

There is no denying that eBay is a platform where you can strike it lucky to get the sports cards you are after. But if you feel, at any point, that the price does not seem right, do the required homework and ask questions. The scammers are just waiting to take advantage of your emotions.

Sales, blow-outs, and being overly pushy

Time is the enemy of any person engaged in unethical practices. They count on buyers to make decisions at a whim and unscrupulously push them to take advantage of the sale.

You have a set budget in mind, and you want to receive joy out of the hobby. Therefore, take your time to do the required research. Often, you will find that all the items listed for sale by this seller are deemed urgent. But do the homework first before buying any sports cards from them.

The correct way to log in to your eBay profile

Don't ever make use of any platform feature, for that matter, whereby the site offers to remember your password automatically. Also, don't bookmark any site as a favorite.

Make a point of logging in from a fresh or incognito tab, entering the link of the site you want to visit. Fraudsters will share a fake link taking you to the site in question and requesting you to log in, in an attempt to use phishing tactics and obtaining your confidential login details.

Direct transactions outside of platforms such as eBay

In an attempt to remain off the radar, a con artist might message you directly to ask if you would consider buying their sports cards away from the platform, or some might even be bold enough to state this on their product descriptions.

There are only one of two reasons that someone might ask you to do this. The first is that they don't want to pay the fees associated with eBay, or they are trying to mislead you. Trying to sell outside of eBay is against their policies.

However, there are legitimate reasons for sellers wanting to ask you to transact outside of the platform. Two such reasons are:

1. eBay does not trade in that person's country of residence, or
2. There is an issue with their eBay shopping cart.

If you have traded with this seller before, you might choose to transact directly, using PayPal. PayPal provides adequate buyer protection, similarly to eBay. You only need to ensure that the goods you are buying are legit, and you need to provide an address to ship to.

Pro-tip: If you engage in a sports card transaction outside of the eBay platform, you can't leave any form of feedback for the seller and afford them any form of credible sales history.

READING THE SPORTS CARD DESCRIPTIONS WITH AN EAGLE EYE

When you make a point of carefully reading every listing's description and comparing it, sellers that have a positive rating might afford you some additional protection against cyber fraud and can help you get the card for your dream sports card portfolio or collection.

Our Tips for Reading Sports Card Descriptions

The actual description of the sports card you want to buy is probably the most crucial factor. This is the perfect opportunity for the seller to provide granular information to prospective sellers on their product for sale.

You should look out for what is and is not being said before going ahead.

The first discussion point is not to judge a seller from the get-go, meaning that if the sentences are written in full, with clear grammar, instructions, etc., the chances are that they took great effort in compiling the listing. There is a tremendous amount of effort and planning that goes into creating the perfect listing.

You should also listen to your gut to determine if you will be comfortable and confident dealing with this particular seller. Some of them are only interested in a quick and dirty transaction, while others value people and prefer to build relationships with their buyers on a professional level.

When sellers list more than one image of their products, it is worth your time to review the whole slideshow before making a decision. Also, watch out for any questions posed to the sellers by other prospective buyers.

Any seller that is worth their salt will engage with buyers frequently and respond to questions. If they don't answer, it does not necessarily raise a red flag. Still, you will then have the responsibility to reach out to the seller via the eBay messaging system and then having them respond to you accordingly.

Some questions you might want to ask:

- Is the item new or used?
- Is the sports card an original print or a reissue?

- Is the card still in its original packaging?
- How long does the seller take to ship the sports card to you?
- Does the shipping amount seem fair to you?
- If the sports card has been graded, does the seller have the necessary certification to prove it?
- Consider the weight of the item vs. the shipping charges you will be expected to pay.
- Make use of a tracking system as far as possible.

Other things to look out for might include if a seller has many spelling and grammar errors, etc., you might want to ask more questions if you really want that particular sports card for your collection or portfolio. But, first, check if there are no other items from other sellers.

eBay needs the seller to advise precisely how they plan on shipping the item. Look under the *Shipping and Payments* tab to see if a shipping charge is actually applicable in this instance and also how much you can expect to pay for it. Some sellers prefer to use eBay's shipping calculator to estimate shipping charges.

Seasoned eBay sports card buyers will tell you that any imperfection on a sports card might be worth risking a bit. But it can also mean the difference between the worth and your bidding price allocated.

BUILDING A POSITIVE SELLERS EBAY RATING

eBay's extensive method of feedback and the prosperity of your e-commerce endeavors are very much dependent on the input and ratings that your buyers provide and any other individual's personal interaction with your listings. When you strive for a higher rating, it will add credibility and will aid you in ranking higher in eBay's analytics search results.

Buyers can rate you on these four components for sports cards sold:

1. The accuracy of the card that you shipped to them.
2. The openness of your communication from start to finish.
3. How long you took to ship the item to them.
4. What you charge for handling and shipping charges.

As a seller, you are also privy to added rewards, such as listing advantages and fee discounts to increase your profit. When you are a seller with a lower rating, your customers might think twice about purchasing sports cards from you, and this could result in you losing your account.

Ultimately, you want to be successful in all of your sales. Subsequently, you should always try to receive a 100% successful feedback rate and a five star rating in each of the aforementioned components. This might be challenging to master as a seller, but you can take measures to ensure that you always obtain the highest level of feedback possible.

Some ways that can help speed up positive ratings include:

Supplying detailed and accurate listing descriptions

Any negative feedback can be avoided by sticking to any promises you made, shipping the items off by the indicated date, and ensuring it is the correct sports card the buyer paid for. Buyers hold an accurate sports card description in high regard. If your product looks good on paper, but you don't deliver as promised, you will receive negative feedback.

If your sports card has any flaws, please ensure that you make mention thereof and take images to show your buyers. If your sports card is not in mint condition and it hasn't been graded, then don't advertise it as such. Your buyers need to know what bang they are getting for their buck, and this way, they won't be disappointed upon receiving the shipment. Taking the time to be specific and honest about your sports cards in the listing description will positively affect your profile as a seller.

Ask your buyers for feedback

A big grievance of sellers within the eBay community is that many of their buyers don't leave them feedback to add some form of credibility to their profile. In most cases, the buyers who are quick to leave feedback have had some type of negative experience from their dealings with the seller. If this has happened to you, the best way to mitigate the situation is to ask them for feedback.

Every time you have successfully completed a sale, reach out to your sports card buyer and ask them for their input on the experience they had with you. Also, ask them for ways in how you can improve your customer service delivery in the future. Kindly request them to chat with you directly if they were not happy and ask them to leave a positive rating if they were satisfied with the service you offered.

This will proactively help you to achieve positive feedback from your happy buyers who have perhaps forgotten to supply you with any feedback. At the same time, it will implore other buyers to speak to you directly when there are issues before leaving a bad review.

It might be a cumbersome task if you have many sports cards to sell, but it will pay off in the long run by securing you a positive rating and high ranking in the eBay sports card trading community.

Effective Communication

As already mentioned, it is vital to have honest and transparent communication with all your buyers to obtain a good relationship with them. After every transaction, ask them if all was in order, including the shipping and receipt of their sports card. Make a point of reaching out before they can take it to eBay to log a negative experience.

If you think you might face any hurdles that will negatively impact your sports card buyers, try to communicate this as soon as possible. Tackle any concerns or questions with potential buyers straight away to build a positive reputation online for effective communication.

This will make your sports card buyer feel valuable, and it will show them that you care and take an interest in their experience. Doing so will result in positive seller ratings before you know it.

Don't delay shipping the sports cards

Your response time for handling and shipping charges can mean a big difference between a positive and a negative rating on eBay. When one of your sports cards is sold, you should ship that card off without delay. This will also increase your seller ratings if the buyers receive their parcels on time. Stay in constant contact with your sports card buyer so that they are aware when the item was dispersed or if you suspect/receive communication that could result in any delays.

It is essential to ship any sold sports cards immediately, but it is equally important to ensure that they are packaged well for the journey to the buyer. If you don't do the required checks in a bid to save money, your customer won't be satisfied, they will wait long for their sports card, and you won't receive a positive rating on your seller's profile.

Respond to any negative ratings

If you perhaps receive negative input or a negative rating from a sports card buyer, contact that buyer and check if there is something that you can do to mitigate the situation. Whether it be sending them another card or merely addressing their concerns, it can make a significant impact on your ratings. If you manage to save the situation, you can then reach out to them again and see if they would be willing to update their previously negative response.

Consider using multi-channel software or consignors

Selling sports cards on eBay can be tiring, and it might be challenging to keep up with all the listings and the components involved in an attempt to reach a high rating as a seller.

The good news is that you can optimize and streamline the entire selling process for your sports cards on eBay. You can either make use of consignors or multi-channel software like Listing Mirror. The API of Listing Mirror is so dynamic, that it can be integrated into various platforms.

These companies can help you to increase positive seller ratings quickly as they facilitate the entire ordering process and organize any inventory on your behalf. These software platforms assist you by creating proper sports card descriptions and listings.

In turn, these listings can be published on many different channels, including eBay for one. It even proactively monitors your inventory and shares tracking numbers to your eBay profile so that your buyers can have an indication as to when they will receive their parcels.

Add a handwritten note to the buyer's parcel

Never underestimate the power of a hand-written note to each of your buyers. This might seem retro to you at first, but this can mean the difference between a good and a great rating on eBay and other platforms.

BUILDING A POSITIVE BUYERS EBAY RATING

Pay promptly and without delay

Strengthen the feedback received from sellers by paying for the sports card immediately after you win an auction or choose the *Buy Now* option. Sellers don't like to ask or wait for their money from buyers.

Paying immediately will also increase your chances of receiving a positive rating. If you are a newbie in the sports card trading community on eBay, bolster your ratings from sellers by purchasing a few low-priced items or sports cards in an attempt to build credibility. All the factors pertaining to building credibility has been discussed on the previous page.

Give the seller feedback straight away

If you are starting in the sports card trading world, it might be hard to try and empathize with the seller you bought the sports card from. They rely heavily on feedback and favorable ratings from their sports card buyers.

Even if you plan to gift the sports card, remove it from the packaging, inspect it and then take it to eBay to write a review. It will only take 30 seconds out of your day. This should be applied no matter what your experience with the seller was. If you were unhappy with the product or service give the seller the chance to rectify the situation and contact them directly before just posting a negative rating.

AN OVERVIEW OF DISCORD GROUPS

Introduction to Discord

The rise of Discord was aimed at solving a common worldwide issue amongst the online gaming community while playing online. It has expanded to the point where different people with different interests have joined the Discord community at the time of writing this article. Some of these include study groups and hiking clubs, among others.

The platform has grown to 100 million active users every month, with an average talk time online daily for four hours and upwards. Discord is the new kid on the block where like-minded individuals chat with each other, network, and just hang out with friends, family, and other community members that share the same interests.

Discord and the Sports Card Trading Community

Sports Card Investor's Mark Ransom and Card Optic are two active admins on their Discord server and endeavor to have a personal relationship with each member who joins their groups. They absolutely love what they do!

Not only do they pride themselves on being active members and administrators, but Sports Card Investor has also fostered a continuous improvement culture to make your experience as a sports card trader more pleasurable and optimized.

Going back to Discord, itself, the server was first developed for the online gaming community. Groups of players playing the same game can then chat via audio or via messaging in an effective, fast and fun way with each other, all while indulging in a game of Rainbow Six Siege or similar games.

Other arts, culture, and recreational groups quickly caught on to the concept and sought a similar product to Discord for gamers. As a sports card collector or investor, the value for you comes in the form of the many channels and subgroups that Sportscardinvestor.com presents to their community of sports card enthusiasts.

They have channels for:

1. Baseball
2. Basketball
3. Football
4. Hockey
5. Soccer
6. Pokemon
7. Razz
8. Live Breaks
9. Selling
10. Premium (paid) channels

Contained in each of these channels are subcategories such as:

- Buy-sell-trade forums
- Grading assistance
- Investment discussions
- Mail day
- New purchases
- New releases

All of their channels are carefully scrutinized for any fraudulent or scamming activity and are a great platform to connect with sellers and breakers and people who love the hobby as much as you do.

This channel serves as an interactive portal where you can join the sports card collecting community and see their opinions in real-time—meaning that you will have up to the minute news at your fingertips that will be highly beneficial to you.

In 2020, after the basketball season is complete, were many exciting discussions amongst their members about who they want to invest in the 2021 season. Even the guys at Sports Card Investor use Discord to research any of their picks and value the opinion of hundreds of other investors like them.

Sports Card Investor's Discord Base

The Sports Card Investor server comprises thousands of active members. Each day sees an influx of newbies signing on to their community. The server currently has between 175 to 200 investors on the platform at any given time of day. The estimated breakdown is more or less 150 sports card investors and more than 1200 members.

Look at it this way; you can ask a question on a platform with more than 1500 members, the administrators, the moderators, and the Sports Card Investor team any day. However, many of their current members have not used this platform to its full potential. You can literally have answers to your questions in mere seconds from posing your question to the community.

Many sports and other celebrities follow the Sports Card Investor community, and you might be lucky enough that one day you get a chance to hear directly from your sports hero. They are passionate about the sports card trading community, and when someone on the platform questions the authenticity of the sports star, they have to share a selfie on the group to prove it is them.

Even if you are not yet confident enough to pose questions, you can learn a lot from just observing and being part of their community on Discord.

How to Start Discording

If you don't already have Discord as an app on your computer, you can search for Discord in your browser and just follow the steps. The mobile version of the app is available on your native app store too.

We would suggest first becoming a member before attempting to upload the mobile version, easing the process. Once you are registered, join the Sports Card Investor community and other sports card-related communities that might interest you.

You can engage directly with any member of the Discord group by hovering over their username. You also have the option to start a discussion with your new-found friends as time goes by. You only need to create a dialogue on the channel of your choice and start typing your message. Monitor the various discussion boards and receive replies in seconds. The version is the same on mobile and web app (on your pc), so the instructions will be the same.

Don't be scared to use the community as support

You need not be intimidated by the technology behind Discord nor by the interface through which you interact with your community. The Sports Card Investor's team is on deck to help you as much as they can. They will even help you to get started and will give you their expert opinion for all scenarios, even if you just use it for research purposes without asking a single question or actively participating.

There is absolutely no obligation to interact or feel pressured in any way. They go above and beyond for their community.

BOX BREAKERS

This is one form of sports card trading that seems to be gaining popularity in the community. It is also referred to as card breaking in some instances. It is a concept not fully understood by Joe Public.

The idea thereof has been making the rounds since the mid-2000s. The precise description of a box or a case break will differ from one breaker to another as each individual has their own way of performing the act of breaking.

The premise of card/box breaking

Generally, it's a sports card collector that streams live on different platforms in the hopes of selling you part of a complete box.

They have to open the box live and then ship the card to you after receiving payment. For example, in the case of the NFL, there are 32 teams in total, and they sell one team per person, and you will then receive the cards pulled from that team in the box that was opened live.

It's a box of sports cards divided between sports card collectors who purchase the right to receive cards as part of this live draw. The concept of raffling is similar, except that each trader is guaranteed a specified number of sports cards.

The idea of hosting this live or replaying it via YouTube at a later stage is to provide sports card collectors with the unique and exciting opportunity of being present as the breaker pulls the cards from the box and does the reveal.

This is a fantastic opportunity for sports card and sports memorabilia collectors to find and buy valuable cards at a price they can afford. It is an exhilarating feeling that cannot be described, but one rather felt when you had experienced it for yourself.

The various versions of box breaking:

Sports card collectors get to choose a pack number from the box and view it being opened live via streaming.

Sports card enthusiasts pick their team in the case or box break. Every team will be priced differently, based on the checklist for the box.

In the event of a random drawing, a randomizer tool is used to determine what is called a draft order. When all the cards have been pulled from a box, the sports card collector's name on the top of the list gets to pick a card/pack first. The process continues on this premise until all the cards have been pulled from the case or the box.

Pros and Cons of Group Breaks

Pros

- You have the opportunity to purchase cards for between $50 and $70 from a box or a case with a total worth of $180 and upwards.
- It is immensely entertaining to watch this event live.
- You can try to negotiate with another sports card collector and trade players or teams with them.
- There is healthy competition and banter amongst the participants, and you can get the opportunity to meme them or send a sympathy card as a joke.
- You might get lucky and get more value from a few cards at a lower price than you would've paid for the entire box.
- There are plenty of bargains up for grabs on the eBay group breaks.
- With group breaking events, you have a better chance of getting more cards if you aim at collecting teams instead of individual players.

Cons

- There is a chance that you might not get any cards at all.
- If lady luck is not on your side, you might be stuck with the runt of the pickings, and then you won't be able to sell or trade with anyone.
- Extra group break fees apply, such as sorting, shipping, and packaging, amongst others.
- There is a risk of encountering a shady breaker and getting ripped off in the process, and paying more for cards than they are actually worth.

The Top 50 Breakers in the industry and their details

- *A&N Sports Cards*
  Twitter: @aandnsportscard
  Website: aansportscards.com

- *All In Cards*
  Twitter: @allincards
  Website: allincards.net

- *Beckett Auctions*
  Twitter: @beckettauctions
  Website: beckett.com/auctions/casebreaks

- *BH35 Sportscards*
  Twitter: @ big_hurt35
  Website: bh35sportscards.com

- *Big Hit Breaks*
  Twitter: @bighitbreaks
  Website: BigHitBreaks.net

- *Big Texas Breaks*
  Twitter: @bigtexasbreaks
  Website: bigtexasbreaks.com

- *BlowoutTV*
  Twitter: @BlowoutTV, @CheapFunBreaks
  Website: BlowoutTV.com

- *Bomber Breaks*
  Twitter: @BomberBreaks
  Website: bomberbreaks.com

- *Box Cutter Sports Cards*
  Twitter: @bobbyboxcutter
  Website: boxcuttersportscards.com

- *Breakaway Sports Cards*
  Twitter: @breakaway_sc
  Website: breakawaysc.com

- *BreakerzAnonymous*
  Twitter: @BzAnonymous
  Website: breakerzanonymous.com

- *Bryan's Breaks*
  Twitter: @viking118480
  Website: bryansbreaks.com

- *CardCollectorX Breaks*
  Twitter: @cardfatherX
  Website: CCXBREAKS.com

- *Cards Infinity*
  Twitter: @CardsInfinity
  Website: cardsinfinity.com

- *CloutsnChara*
  Twitter: @Cloutsnchara
  Website: cloutsnchara.com

- *Crackin' Wax*
  Twitter: @CrackinWax
  Website: crackinwax.wordpress.com

- *DACW Live*
  Twitter: @DACWLiveBreaks
  Website: dacardworld.com

- *Downtown Breaks*
  Twitter: @downtownbreaks
  Website: downtownbreaks.com

- *Finest Box Breaks*
  Twitter: @finestboxbreaks
  Website: finestboxbreaks.com

- *Firehand Cards*
  Twitter: @FireHand17
  Website: firehandcards.com

- *Friendly Box Breaks*
  Twitter: @FriendlyBreaks
  Website: friendlyboxbreaks.com

- *GV Sports*
  Twitter: @gvsportscards
  Website: gvsportscards.com

- *Jaspy's Hobbyland*
  Website: jaspyshobbyland.com
  Twitter: @JaspysHobbyLand

- *Jonesy's Sports Cards*
  Twitter: @JonesysSportsBR
  Website: jonesysbreaks.com

- *KennFudd Sports Cards*
  Twitter: @KennFudd
  Website: kennfudd.miiduu.com

- *KT Authentics*
  Twitter: @KTAuthentics
  Website: ktauthentics.com

- *K2 Sports Cards*
  Twitter: @K2SportsCards
  Website: k2sportscards.com

- *Layton Sports Cards*
  Twitter: @RichLayton42
  Website: laytonsportscards.com

- *Live Box Breaks*
  Twitter: @LBBdotNET
  Website: liveboxbreaks.net

- *LiveCaseBreak*
  Twitter: @ LiveCaseBreak
  Website: livecasebreak.com

- *Minera Sports Cards*
  Twitter: @MustashMondays
  Website: minerasportscards.com

- *MojoBreak*
  Twitter: @mojobreak_com
  Website: mojobreak.com

- *NastyBreaks.com*
  Website: nastybreaks.com

- *One of One Box Breaks*
  Twitter: @oneofonebbreaks
  Website: oneofoneboxbreaks.com

- *Out of the Box*
  Twitter: @OutoftheBoxBrks
  Website: outoftheboxcards.com

- *Platinum Card Breaks*
  Twitter: @PlatCardBreaks
  Website: platinumcardbreaks.com

- *RipandList*
  Twitter: @ripandlist
  Website: breakers.tv/ripandlist

- *Rip Kings*
  Twitter: @RIPKINGSRippin
  Website: ripkings.com

- Ripping Wax
  Twitter: @rippingwax
  Website: rippingwax.com

- *RyneM Case Breaks*
  Twitter: @RynemCaseBreaks
  Website: rynemcasebreaks.com

- *Six Eight Cards*
  Twitter: @SixEightCards
  Website: sixeightcards.com

- *Sports Box Breaks*
  Twitter: @SBBTweet
  Website: sportsboxbreaks.com

- *Steel City Collectibles*
  Twitter: @SCCTradingCards
  Website: steelcitycollectibles.com

- *STL Sports Cards*
  Twitter: @STLSportsCards
  Website: mystlsportscards.com

- *Supreme Card Breakers*
  Twitter: @supremebreaks
  Website: supremecardbreakers.com

- *The Break King*
  Twitter: @thebreakking
  Website: thebreakking.com

- *The Case Breakers*
  Twitter: @thecasebreakers
  Website: thecasebreakers.com

- *Top Cut Breaks*
  Twitter: @TopCutBreaks
  Website: topcutbreaks.com

- *Top Shelf Breaks*
  Twitter: @TopShelfBreaks
  Website: topshelfbreaks.com

- *Ultimate Box Breaks*
  Twitter: @TheUBB
  Website: ultimateboxbreaks.com

OTHER PLACES TO BUY OR SELL SPORTS CARDS

Stock X

Stock X is the first online marketplace that operates on the premise of "bid/ask" prices. A transaction is automatically done by adjoining the bids placed by sports card buyers, and the ask comes from the sports card sellers.

The basics thereof

Stock X works on three business pillars, namely:

- **Anonymity** - Because they are the middleman, neither the seller nor the buyer has to be concerned with a sports card's legitimacy and the persons behind the transaction.

- **Transparency** - The platforms give both sports card buyers and sellers access to real-time market data.
- **Authenticity** - Every transaction is vetted by the Stock X team.

How to buy sports cards on Stock X

1. Make an offer to a seller that they can accept or purchase a sports card at the lowest asking price.
2. The seller ships the card to Stock X, they authenticate the card, and then sends the funds to the seller.
3. Once the vetting process is complete, Stock X ships the card to the buyer.

How to sell sports cards on Stock X

1. List a sports card or accept an offer from a buyer at the highest price.
2. After the sale is complete, ship the sports card to Stock X for vetting.
3. After the authentication process is complete, Stock X releases your funds.

The Pit

This company has placed emphasis on rookie cards of both current players and then graded retro cards from Hall of Famers.

How to trade on The Pit

In as little as three steps, you can now also join The Pit community:

1. Create a free account on the site.
2. Navigate through the site for player cards that you want to collect or add to your investment portfolio.

3. Add the details of your sports trading cards for others to trade with you. Guess what? There are no trading fees attached. You can enjoy a cash-out at lower fees than some of their competitors, or you can request shipment, and their team will ship the sports cards to you 48 hours after the transaction has concluded.

comc.com

Check Out My LLC. (Check Out My Collectibles), or COMC for short has been in existence since 2005. They use the latest technology available to optimize the lives of sports card traders across the world.

The reasons why you should buy on COMC

They offer flat-rate shipping options

With their "buy now, ship later" product on offer, you can buy sports cards from many sellers over a period of time and choose to ship them all at once and save costs at the same time. An added benefit is that all the cards will arrive in one package.

Having fun

Is this not the reason we are in this hobby? You can use their filters, such as checking for a set, a player, a team, and much more. You have the option of flipping cards, buying instantly, or immediately relisting any sports cards as for sale.

The reasons why you should sell on COMC

They do all of the work for you, such as:

- Doing the required research and then identifying the sports cards you have an interest in and that would add value to your portfolio or collection.
- Evaluating the value and condition of your sports cards that are listed as for sale.
- They scan the back and the front of the card on your behalf.
- They advertise as a proxy on your behalf, leaving you to focus on other things.
- They are responsible for storing and insuring all your collectibles.
- They have the responsibility of facilitating any customer services queries on your behalf.
- They package and ship the sports cards as your proxy and are also responsible for shipping them off to the individual buyers based on their chosen shipping option.

— CHAPTER 6 —

GLOSSARY, ABBREVIATIONS, ACRONYMS AND SLANG WORDS

"That one little piece of paper - at that moment, it was special. The fan and the athlete came together in a special way."
—Dodger first baseman Steve Garvey.

A

Acetate: This is a transparent, clear type of plastic used by trading card producers as a substitute for another, usually more traditional in nature, from other cardboard and paper stock. Trading card manufacturer Upper Deck has made use of this packaging method in their ICE and Trilogy Hockey sports cards.

When you click on the image, you are able to see the details printed on the back of the sports card by viewing it through the front of the sports card.

American Card Catalogue: This is basically dubbed as the Dewey Decimal System in the sports card world and is the brainchild of founding father Jefferson Burdick. He has spent his whole life creating this product, and it is deemed as a standardized form of categorization for sports cards that is still in use today.

Artificial Scarcity: This is a term that describes the practice of sports card producers that intentionally prints certain sports cards in a limited quantity to classify them as rare or scarce.

Airbrush: This is a term used to describe a sports card that has been artificially altered somehow. This was a retro technique that sports card manufacturers employed before the digital age. It operated on the premise whereby a player moved teams, and the then sports card producer did not have an image at their disposal of the player in their new kit. The image from the previous team uniform was altered using a technique called airbrushing.

Artist Proof: This card type belongs to the parallel collection of sports cards. The first sports card producers that made these types of cards were Pinnacle Brands, with the inception year being 1994.

Authenticating an autograph: Also known as Autograph Authentication. This is the method by which a sports card is vetted to determine if the signature is true and is also the signature of the athlete in question.

An autograph: This is a sports card with the signature of the sports personality or athlete. The acronym Auto and AU is also used to describe this sports card.

B

Base card: These numbered cards are the primary cards in a sports card producer's base set.

Base set: All of the sports cards that are made up of a collection of base cards.

BCCG: A service offering by sports card manufacturer Beckett, specifically in the grading of sports cards on a platform called Shop at Home Network.

BCW: This is a maker of display pieces and storage supplies for sports card collecting and other sports-related memorabilia.

Beckett: The producer of sports cards and their respective price guidelines.

BGS: This is the acronym for *Beckett* Grading Services. This is an outlet of *Beckett* that focuses on the grading of sports cards.

BVG: Or, *Beckett* Vintage Grading is an outlet of *Beckett* that grades vintage sports cards.

Big Four: This term bears reference to four of the rarest sports cards in ATC's 1909–11 T206 set that was released. The *Big Four* refers to players Eddie Plank, Honus Wagner, Larry Doyle, and Sherry "Magie."

Bip: A term used by collectors when they receive more than one copy of the same card from one pack in particular.

Black box: This is the party favor that *Panini America* gifts to the participants of an event called the Industry Summit and also at the *Panini* VIP Party after the *National Sports Collectors Convention.*

Blank back: This term describes a sports card with no printing whatsoever on the back of the card. This might be either a design or a printing error. Interestingly enough, they are deemed as being of very high value.

Blaster box: Packs of sports cards packed for big retail chains such as *Target* or *Wal-Mart.* Usually, there are between five to ten packs of cards in such a box and, if you are lucky, you might even score a premium in the process.

Blister pack: This is a form of sports card packaging that comprises a few different packs of sports cards. They range between two to four packs that are then sealed in a hard plastic container with a cardboard back. Recently, it was found that some blister packs might have a few solo cards in their box.

Typically, the standalone cards found in blister packs are parallels that have been wrapped in cellophane. You might even find team sets in blister packs.

Book card: This is a sports card that has been created by joining two separate cards employing a hinge or something similar to a book spine. They can be either horizontally or vertically aligned. They possess unique features such as game-used jerseys and even signatures in some cases. It is also sometimes referred to as a booklet card.

Book value: Be it somewhat of a retro term, but still in use today. It describes a sports card's value in money as listed on a pricing guide published by sports card authenticators like *Beckett*.

Bowman: This was a standalone bubblegum manufacturer that started making sports cards in the mid-40s. Rival company *Topps* acquired them in 1989. *Bowman's* primary focus was on that of rookies and prospects.

Box Break: A term used to describe the act of opening a box of trading cards.

Box Break Site: This is a website that hosts events called Group Breaks.

Box Card: This term refers to a sports card that is found, for example, by digging through a box of cereal as conducted in the 80s. The term panel card is also sometimes used to describe the same term.

Box-topper: This describes what is known as a premium contained within a box of sports trading cards.

Break: This is sports card community lingo for the act of opening up a box of sports cards. Sometimes the terms bust and cracked are used to describe the same act.

Brick: A term used amongst the sports card community of the early 80s. It bears reference to selling a bundle of 50 sports cards and selling them as one product. The practice is not common today.

Brick-and-Mortar: This term describes a physical sports card trading store that sells sports cards online retailer of sports cards.

Buyer's premium: The percent charged by auction houses to a winning bidder of a sports card. This is to cover both the profit margin and expenses of the auction house.

C

Cabinet card: This term refers to a sports card that is much larger than the average size. In the 19th and 20th centuries, sports card enthusiasts used to display them in cabinets known as Curios to show them off and for it to serve as a display piece in their homes and offices. The cabinet was deemed as part of the furniture. Hence the name cabinet card was born.

Card stock: Refers to the material the card is made from.

Cardboard Connection: This is a website that sells sports cards and other sports memorabilia.

Case: This is a form of sports card packing containing between two and 20 boxes of sports cards.

Case Breaker: A person or an operation that breaks cases containing boxes of sports cards.

Case hit/hits: This is when sports card producers sell cases of sports cards and can then guarantee short-printed cards or cards of a high value.

Category: Sports card enthusiasts use this term to describe the sports card market from both a hobby and a retail perspective.

Cello: This can refer to either boxes or packs. It describes the act of wrapping sports cards in a material that resembles cellophane from the 70s to the 90s. The term rack packs also apply to this term as these packs had holes so they could be hung in stores from racks.

Chase set: An alternative card used as a substitute to an insert card.

Checklist: A list containing all of the sports cards that can be found in base-, insert-, and subsets of products.

Chrome: A type of sports card made by Topps. It has a beautiful metallic finish and sheen on the surface.

Collated: A term that describes the end-to-end process of how sports cards are distributed in the product run.

Collector's corner: A digital platform that sells sports cards that have been authenticated by sports card authenticator PSA.

Collector revolution: The term used to describe another digital platform that serves as a substitute to *eBay,* where sports cards can be traded between members of the sports card community.

C.O.A: Or, a Certificate of Authenticity describes the legitimacy of a sports card. They are published and sent to the owner of the sports card by one of the sports card authenticators, such as PSA, to certify features, such as the signature of an athlete or any uniform that has been used in a game by the player in question.

COMC: A company called Check Out My Collectibles. This is a digital platform where sports card buyers and sellers can trade cards.

Commemorative: A sports card that has been created in celebration of a special event.

Common/commons: This refers to the cards contained in a set that are the cheapest.

Completist: This is a sports card collector or investor that endeavors to complete a set or collect all of the sports cards ever manufactured from a particular team or player.

Condition: Refers to a sports card's features that determine the quality thereof using a conditioning scale.

Conditioning issues: This term describes all of the flaws of a sports card that will affect its value, especially in the instance of grading.

Conditioning scale: This is a list of naming conventions that refer to a sports card's condition and its quality.

Cut case: The act whereby *Topps* wanted to rid their inventory of excess sports cards in the 70s and 80s.

Cut signature. An auto from an athlete that has been cut from a large document

D

Dealer: A buyer or seller of trading cards, among other collectibles, to generate income. In the past, the term referred to those that advertised a local geographic market of collectibles. However, the online markets have made collectors become dealers.

Death Bump: A temporary rise in collectibles' value related to a celebrity or athlete that dies.

Diamond Border or Cut: A trading card featuring a border design that is unparalleled to the card's edges. Such is the case of the 2010 *Topps* T-206 mini-Chrome that features the legendary Honus Wagner.

Diamond Certified Dealer: An *Upper Deck* program designating and rewarding the company's dealers that hit the target criteria and sales goals.

Die-Cut: A trading card with one of its parts. It has a specific design, function, or shape. Currently, such cards apply as inserts. They are also rare due to short-printing.

Ding/Dinged Corner: A damage that appears on the trading card's corner due to the card's mishandling. It has a lower value than a card without a ding.

Distributor: A wholesale middleman between a retailer and a manufacturer. They provide services such as sales promotions and marketing support to drive sales.

- *Major Distributors*: They include *GTS Distribution, Peach State*, and *Southern Hobby Supply*.

Doctored/Doctoring: An altered trading card. The altering offers a cover-up. The process includes trimming, flattening, and building up. It is a flaw to hobby purists.

- *Trimmed*: The removal of some parts of a trading card.
- *Built-up*: The creation of artificial corners using corn starch.
- *Flattened*: Removing creases from the surface of a card using a teaspoon.

Donruss: An entertainment trading cards manufacturer that began operations in the 1950s. Their production of sports cards began in 1981. The company has changed hands several times. Currently, *Panini* America owns the company.

Double Print (DP): A trading card with double the number of cards than other cards within a set.

Dufex: A manufacturing patent from the defunct *Pinnacle Brands Inc*. It features a reflective quality that appears as a foil-layer coating on a card. It was popular among the collectors due to its unique quality.

Dump or Product Dumping: A quick elimination of unwanted inventory by discounting its price. Also, see MAPP.

E

Emboss, Embossing, or Embossed: Pressing an image, design, or text to indent a paper card using a printing process.

Encapsulated: A card with a permanent and tamper-resistant plastic case seal. It is one of the outcomes of authentication of grading. However, some of the current high-end cards are encapsulated.

Entertainment Trading Cards: Trading cards with entertainment subjects, such as movies and TV shows, rather than sports subjects.

- *Non-Sport Trading Cards:* Used to replace the term "entertainment trading cards." However, the hobby has been using the terms interchangeably according to the type of trading card.

Ephemera: Any paper that is a collectible, such as trading cards, postcards, and yearbooks.

Error Card: A trading card with an error, such as a misspelling or the wrong photograph. If the error is corrected, then it becomes a *Corrected Error Card*. Printing in smaller quantities determines the card will have a premium value.

- *No Name On Front (NNOF):* Such as the 1990 *Topps* baseball card featuring Frank Thomas. Initially, it missed a name. However, it was distributed; thus, it's carrying a premium after the correction of the error.

eTopps: A 2000 *Topps'* online trading card with a design that leveraged on the increasing internet popularity. The company sold the cards as IPOs (Initial Player Offering) only for one week.

Exhibit Card: A trading card with a size similar to that of a postcard. The Exhibit Card Company produced and distributed the card between the 1920s and 1960s.

Extended Rookie Card (XRC): A term from the price guide publications designating a card that a player used during his or her rookie year. It is not part of the standard base set. The card had a limited edition, and was popular in the hobby from the 80s to the early 90s.

F

Facsimile Signature: An autograph done on a trading card using a stamp or the overall printing process. It is an imitation of an original autograph made by a subject.

Factory Set: A complete trading card set that a manufacturer packages. It carries a premium, unlike the hand-collated sets.

Flat: The "flat" memorabilia items that are to be autographed. They include photographs, books, and magazines.

- *Premium Item:* An item with a surface that is not flat, to be autographed. They include jerseys and balls.

Fleer: A trading card from the defunct *New Jersey Trading Card Company*. Currently, *Upper Deck* owns it.

Foil: Shiny, metallic-like film used on trading cards. The addition of the film is one of the printing process steps.

Foil Pack/Wrapper: They replaced the 1990s wax wrappers. *Upper Deck* introduced the metallic foil in 1989.

Food Issue: A trading card used as a premium during the distribution of food products, such as Post Cereal and Holsum Bread.

Forum: An online community of collectors to discuss hobbies, find information, make trades, and get peer feedback.

- *Board or Message Board:* Similar to the forum.
- *Moderator:* The overseeing person in a forum to prevent abusive language and other violations of the forum's policies.
- *Popular Message Boards:* They include *Sports Card Forum, Beckett, Freedom Cardboard, Traders Central,* and *NET54*.

Full Bleed: A printing term describing a borderless trading card. The printing covers the entire face of a cardboard.

G

Game-Used: Memorabilia from a past professional sporting event. They include basketball nets, bases, hockey sticks, and bats.

Game-Worn: Memorabilia that a player wore in an actual game. They include shoes, hats, pads, and jerseys.

- *Player-Worn:* Memorabilia that a player wore but not during a game. They include a jersey worn during a photoshoot.
- *Photoshoot Worn:* Memorabilia that a player wore explicitly for a photoshoot.
- *Event Used:* Memorabilia that a player wore during a specific event, such as the Draft day.

Gavel Price: The final selling value of an item at an auction without including the buyer's premium.

Gem Card: Trading cards with genuine gemstones. They are also known as Jewel Cards. They appear in various brands, including *Panini* and *Upper Deck*.

Gimmick Card: A derogatory term for cards made by a company with little knowledge on true collectability. It is made for the hype of media attention—for example, the 2007 *Topps* Card featuring Derek Jeter. However, the card is varied to include George W. Bush.

Gloss/Glossy: A card with a shiny luster from the application of UV coating during the printing process.

Graded Card: A graded card with a specific numerical grade depicting its physical condition.

Grading Company: An independent third party that examines a trading card and assigns a numerical grade depicting the card's physical condition. They include *Beckett Grading Services (BGS)*, *Global Authentication Inc. (GAI)*, and *Professional Sports Authenticators (PSA)*.

Graded/Grading Card Scale: A numerical scale that individual grading companies use. It is mostly 1–10. However, only SCG uses 10–100. The numbers depict the physical condition of a card.

- *Pristine*: A BGS term for grade 10.
- *Gem Mint:* A PSA term describing grade 10.

Please refer to the specific grading scale for each company for more information.

- *Qualifier:* Condition issues used to determine the merit of a card for a specific grade.
- *Off-Center* (OC): The centering of a lower card than the minimum standard related to that grade.
- *Stained/Staining (ST)*: Cards bearing stains below the minimum standard related to that grade.
- *Print Defect (PD)*: Cards bearing several printing defects.
- *Out of Focus (OF)*: Cards bearing a photographic focus below the minimum standard related to that grade.

- *Marks (MK)*: Cards with impression evidence from writing using ink or pencil.
- *Miscut (MC)*: Cards featuring cuts that do not align with a particular set's standard dimension.

Gravity Feed: A retail packaging method that makes the bottom of the box to have an opening for accessing the cards. The sealed, tall, and rectangular boxes hold 48, 72, or 96 packs.

Group Break: An opportunity for a "group" of collectors to come together online and split the cost of a box or case of cards and then divide the pulled cards amongst themselves in a manner that was previously agreed upon before the break begins.

- *Random Break:* A spot for all teams. For example, the NFL has 32 spots, meaning that there are 32 teams and 32 participants. After filling all spots, randomization occurs, paring each numbered team with a participant.
- *Pre-Priced Team:* A predetermined price that applies to each team. The high-value cards or "hits" determine the price. Additionally, the number of Stars, HOF'ers, and Rookies also determines the price.
- *Hit Draft:* "Hits" on sports cards that do not have insert or base cards. So, 20 cards can only have 20 participants. The Random Break mentioned above sets the draft order. The randomization ranking provides the order of picking the cards. That is the first player, after randomization, picks the first card, and so on.
- *Live Auction:* An auction that starts with the minimum price of a team. It occurs in the break room, and each team gets the card that it wins (and purchased).

- *Divisional:* All sport divisions that a product being broken possesses. The break can either be draft or random style. However, both styles are conducted similarly to how the draft break of traditional random is undertaken. Afterward, participants own all the teams in the division related to that break.
- *Team Draft:* A randomizer determines the draft order. The first player gets the first draft pick. The "on the clock" participant chooses the remaining teams. A selection allocates you to a team in that particular break.
- *Razz:* A group break with more team slots than its actual teams. It has questionable legality, and many sites do not use the practice.

Gum Stain: A stain made by chewing gum on a card. It occurs on the top and bottom card packed next to chewing gum when the pack remains unopened for a long time. The stain devalues the affected card.

H

Hall of Fame Inductee: A player that gets an induction from their respective hall of fame related to their sports.

- *HOF'er:* Hall of Fame player
- *HOF:* Hall of Fame

Hanger Box: A replacement for blaster boxes to conserve shelf space in big-box retailer stores. A hanger box contains assorted and unopened packs similar to a blaster box. It also hangs from a display in a store.

High Numbers: A term that applies to vintage cards printed before 1973 describing the last, or near-the-last cards, of a trading set. They belong to the last print run, last distributed print cards, and last released series.

High Series, High Number Series, or High Number: The last trading cards in the last printed series. Their distribution is in a set within a given year.

For years, manufacturers distributed trading cards in "series." The reducing interest towards the end of a sports season resulted in the printing of smaller quantities. The reduced production increased the value of other cards within the set.

Hit or Hit Card: A term from the modern hobby for high-valued cards, or those perceived as of higher value than the rest of the cards in a trading cards box. Such cards may be autographed, highly short-printed, or have memorabilia.

Hobby Box: An exclusively packaged box of trading cards distributed through approved traditional card shops and online retailers.

- *Retail Box:* Packaged for sale and distribution at large retail outlets and chains like Wal-Mart and Target. The contents of the two types of boxes often vary, with Hobby Boxes typically having better insert odds and sometimes different content altogether.

  These establishments' buying power has generated demand for Retail-Only products or those with exclusive content in recent years.

Hobby Only/Exclusive: Interchangeable terms referring to product, packaging configuration, and product content with an exclusive design for distribution via hobby channels.

Hologram: A printing technology for creating a reflective, 3D-like effect. It is also a specific hologram that the authentication process applies. *Upper Deck* introduced it in 1989 to fight counterfeiting. Currently, other companies, such as *Panini,* are using it.

- *Hologram Card:* A trading card with part or whole holographic image. For example, The Pinnacle hologram card of 1966.

Home Team Advantage (HTA): A late 1990s *Topps* promotional program. It features specific types of packs and exclusive products found in the participating Hobby Stores.

Hot Box: A current trading card term describing a box with high-end cards only, "Hits" only, or extra bonus content.

Hot Pack: It has two meanings according to their manufacturing era: 1) A 1990s pack from the *Fleer* company containing inserts only. 2) Presently, a pack is guaranteed to feature memorabilia or an autograph. They are found on *eBay,* but their contents remain debatable.

I

Industry Summit: An annual tradeshow in the trading card industry. The show evolved from the Hawaii Trade Convention.

Ink Analysis: The process of authenticating the ink used to make an autograph to identify the signature's specific period.

Inscribed/Inscription: A specialized notation beside the autograph of a subject. The notation can be the statistical achievement or nickname.

Insert Card: All non-parallel and non-base cards within a trading card set. Such cards have unique names, themes, numbering, and designs.

Insert Odds: The insert cards in each number of packs. For example, 1:4 means one in four packs.

Issue: A reference for a trading card set in association with its manufacturer. For example, the 1975 *Topps* Mini issue.

J

Jersey (JSY): The upper-body part of the uniform of a player.

Jersey Card: A trading card with a part of a jersey material. It is also called the swatch.

Jewel Card: A trading card with genuine gemstones. For example, *Lillard's* 2012–13 flawless Rookie card from *Panini*. They are only 20. The gem appears next to the serial numbering.

Jumbo Pack: An exclusive trading pack consisting of more cards than the regular retail versions, such as the ones manufactured by *Bowman Baseball* and *Topps*. They contain 50–60 sports cards.

Junk Wax: The majority of the trading cards manufactured between the 80s & early 90s. There was overproduction during the period making the cards making them have little or no monetary value.

Just Minors: A defunct trading manufacturer that printed specific trading card sets featuring minor league teams and respective players.

K

Key: A designation of the most important cards within a set, rookies of a certain draft class year, or players appearing on a checklist.

Krause: A long-serving hobby publisher that produces the annual Sports Cards Standard Catalogs featuring the memorabilia price guides and the *Sports Collectors* digest weekly issues. The publisher is a subsidiary of *F+W Media*.

L

Letter of Authenticity: Or, sometimes called an L.O.A, is a formal written letter sent by a sports card authenticator to the owner of a sports card stating that they have authenticated as legitimate.

It lists detailed and granular information on the card and is signed by the authenticator who performed the vetting and the third-party company president.

Leaf: A 1930s trading card manufacturer. It has changed hands several times, and *Panini America* bought it in 2009. The company now operates as the *Leaf Trading Cards* under *Razor Entertainment.*

Lenticular: A printing technology with a 3D effect that gives images a movement appearance when viewed from different angles.

Licensed: A trading card with authorized usage rights and official endorsement from a sports licensing body, such as NBA and NHL.

Limited Edition: A term implying scarcity of a product. Such a product has a value that corresponds with the exact quantity of production. Oversupply lowers the value of a card.

Limited Production Run: A description of a product's total print run, especially when its quantity is lower than that of the rest of the products.

Live Ink: Real ink on an item other than photocopy or stamp.

Loupe/Jewelers Loupe: A small, high-powered tool that magnifies autographs, printing patterns, jersey stitching on printed items. Some premium loupes use UV light to uncover any form of card doctoring.

Lot: A number of items to be used in bidding. They include trading cards. They may be similar or assorted.

Low Series, Low Number Cards: Cards belonging to the first print run. They are distributed as a set within a given year. Their production and distribution are high due to the high demand during the start of a sports season.

M

Manufacturer: A sports and entertainment company that produces memorabilia and trading cards.

Manufactured Relic: A player-worn or non-game used item that a producing company physically manufactures in a limited manner. It comes as an insert or premium in a product related to a trading card—for example, coins, pins, charms, and rings.

Master Set: A complete cards print run including parallel, insert, and base cards with memorabilia and autographs.

- *Related Term: Mini-Master Set -* A complete cards print run including parallel, insert, and base cards without memorabilia and autographs (parallels are the exception).

Minimum Advertised Pricing Program (MAPP): A pricing policy that trading card manufacturers instituted to curb product dumping and wholesale and direct dealer underpricing. The policy sets the minimum price of a product for a specific period.

Memorabilia Authentication: The special services that assess the genuineness and authenticity of game-used and game-worn memorabilia, including jerseys, balls, helmets, and bats. The assessment results from the market demand for genuine sports memorabilia.

Related Term(s)

- *Bat Card:* A relic card featuring a baseball bat piece, also known as a bat "chip."
- *Bat Barrel Card:* A memorabilia card featuring a part of a bat's barrel, especially that part with a player's printed name or the bat's model.
- *Bat Knob Card:* A rare memorabilia card featuring a handle knob of a baseball bat.
- *Coin Card:* A relic card featuring a physical coin.
- *Jersey Card:* A trading card featuring a swatch (A piece of material that makes a jersey).
- *Jersey Swatch:* A single-color section or non-patch section of a jersey material.
- *Jumbo:* A jersey patch or swatch that occupies a large part of a trading card landscape.
- *Nameplate Card:* A card featuring a single letter that comes from the nameplate of a player printed at the backside of the players' uniform.
- *Patch Card:* A jersey card featuring a part of a player's multi-color jersey, especially numerals and logos of a jersey.
- *Prime:* A rare part of memorabilia featuring the unique aspects of a jersey, especially the advertiser of laundry tags.
- *Stamp Card:* A relic card featuring a postage stamp.

Metal/Metallic: A technologically printed card that resembles or features a metallic finish.

Mini: A non-traditional size of a trading card. For example, the 1975 *Topps*-test issue. Recently, the concept has been applied in creating the traditional-sized cards in a set or even the complete set of mini-sized cards.

Mini-Bat: A small-scale baseball replica mainly used for autographs.

Mini-Helmet: A small-scale football helmet replica mainly used for autographs.

Minor League Card: Baseball cards depicting players of the existing minor leagues.

- *Prospect Card:* A card featuring a player belonging to a system minor league but not belonging to a major league's roster.

Mint On Card (MOC): The term for entertainment or sports packaging, such as the starting lineups or the McFarlane Sportspicks.

Multimedia Cards: The recent traditional trading cards that employ digital media.

- *Video Trading Card or Video Card:* Cards that Upper Deck (Evolution) and Panini (HRX) produced in 2012. The cards feature a tiny monitor for playing video highlights that relates to the cards' subject.
- *Power Deck:* A PC-played CD-ROM showing the subject's biography, statistics, and video highlights.

Multiplier: A term from a price guide expressing the value of a card against a popular card. It saves the publication space. For example, the semi-stars 2 x of 1965. Such a card is double the value of a common-base card.

N

National Sports Collectors Convention (NSCC): A memorabilia and sports card annual show started in 1989. It is a unique show because of its number of attendees, exhibitors, corporate partners, and size. Recently, the show has taken place in Cleveland, Baltimore, Atlantic City, and Chicago, interchangeably.

New In Box (NIB): An originally boxed toy, memorabilia, or novelty item.

Notching: Indentions that appear on the edge of a trading card because a rubber band was used to hold the cards together.

Non-Sport Update (NSU): A price guide and hobby publication that occurs bi-monthly focusing on the above entertainment trading cards or non-sports trading cards.

No Purchase Necessary (NPN): An offer to consumers for having the same odds of an insert card from a trading card product without the product's actual purchase. The offers result from adherence to specific laws that govern sweepstakes and other products that feature the odds. Each manufacturer has to print their NPN program terms on the wrappers of a trading card.

Numbering: A card number that indicates the order of the card in a set. It is affixed on the back of a trading card.

- *Serial Numbering:* A stamped number that indicates the exact print run of a card. It appears as xx/xxx (serial number/total number of cards of a similar type). The numbers are standard in insert and parallel cards.

O

Oddball: A collectible affiliated with entertainment or sports that does not belong to any specific category, such as regular cards or other popular collected items. For example, soda or beer cans, product premiums, or any other unique collectible.

On-Card: An autographed card with a direct signature but not with a signature on its sticker label.

- *Hard-Signed:* A term that also describes an On-Card.
- *Sticker Auto or Sticker Autograph:* A card bearing a signature on its sticker or label but not on its actual face. It is the opposite of an On-Card or Hard-Signed card.

One-of-One: A rare trading card with a serial number, such as designation 1/1. Such a designation denotes that there is only one trading card of that nature.

Online Retailer: An online reseller that uses their website to sell memorabilia or trading cards. Such a reseller uses online platforms, such as eBay. Sometimes, such retailers have a physical retail store as well.

P

Pack: A set of cards that a manufacturer packs for sale.

Pack Searcher: A person that tries to locate a pack containing a "hit card" in a retail box containing several packs of cards. They exist among the big-box retailers. Their actions are not encouraged because they remove the chase-fun among other collectors.

Upper Deck is actively lobbying against the practice, and the company is in the process of educating the big box retailers to shun the pack-searching practice.

Paper Analysis: The analysis is significant in document authentication, similar to the above ink analysis. A paper has distinct characteristics, and it is a medium with a very high individualization. Professional examiners have the ability to examine and tell whether a paper belongs to an alleged signing era.

Parallel: A card resembling its counterpart in a base set but with a distinguishing quality, such as texture, color, or printing technology.

Penny Sleeve: A thin plastic pocket used as the first level of card protection. They can also be inserted into a top loader for further protection. Penny sleeves are inexpensive and come in quantities of 100 in a package.

Personal Collection (PC): A modern hobby description of a collection of cards that the holder does not sell or trade. The cards are a part of a personal collection.

Photo-Matching: The act of comparing memorabilia with the photographs that belong to a specified period for authentication. The authenticators compare wear and tear and logo placement, among other features. Photo-matching helped in the authentication of the Payton Manning jersey used in the October 9, 2005 game.

Photo-Shopped: The process of using Adobe's Photoshop to alter a digital image. The process results in trading cards that are not genuine.

Pocket Sheets/Pages: Protective sheets for trading cards. They have an archival quality that does not have any acids and PVCs. They offer ultra-violet protection. Their dimensions fit a standard three-ring binder.

One can also purchase them in configurations that hold standard cards, tobacco cards, 8 x 10 photographs, and other sizes. Their designation is nine pocket sheets that hold the traditional cards.

Population Report: They are a graded number of cards. A specific grading company does grading. The grading also specifies the number of cards in a particular grade.

Premium: An additional item in a trading card box. It is also an increased value of a card or article due to rarity or the above conditional issues, among other factors.

Pre-War/Post-War: World War II is a dividing line that applies to many collectibles. Often, collectibles bear one of the designations.

Price Guides: Print or online third-party publications providing collectors with the current market's trading card estimated value. Prices undergo changes on an ongoing basis and accumulated value from traditional hobby shops and online markets. The card values are also the book value.

- *OPG (Online Price Guide)*: A card values' more extensive offering that appears on the monthly hard copies.

Printing Plate(s): Recent years' printing process' actual plates that have become collectibles. The making of each set of trading cards uses four plates: Cyan, Yellow, Magenta, and Black.

The plates are inserted in packs with serial numbers 1/1.

Prism: A metallic-like quality card with a shiny and bright design. The card refracts and disperses light.

Prizm: A brand name from Panini America describing their specific parallel cards. The cards have a metallic-like quality card with a shiny and bright design. They also refract and disperse light.

Promotional Card: A card produced and distributed to collectors free of charge to promote a trading card's upcoming release. Their small print runs enable them to carry a premium.

They were popular among the sports card manufacturers, but the entertainment trading card manufacturers also use them nowadays. The promotional cards are also called the Promo Cards.

Prop Card or Prop Relic: A memorabilia card featuring a part of a movie or TV show prop. It is found in entertainment trading cards.

Prospect Card: Similar to a Minor League card, a prospect card features a player from a minor league system but not from a major league roster.

Puzzle Card: A card with a part of a picture on its backside. When joined with other puzzle cards, they form a complete picture. *Donruss* pioneered using the puzzle card after a court ruling giving *Topps* the sole right of distributing gum trading cards.

Q

Qualifier: Sometimes, a qualifier determines the designation of a card. A "qualified card" meets all the requirements of a particular grade but fails in the standards of one specific area, such as the NM-MT 8 with a 90/10 left to right-center. Such a card receives an NM-MT 8 (OC) grade, where OC stands as the qualifier.

R

Rack Pack: A configuration of trading card sold through channels of retail. When handed on display, it resembles a set of three single packs. The type of sport and manufacturer determines the number of cards in a rack pack. However, they are more than the quantity of cards in a single card pack.

Rainbow: The entire series that contains all possible colors of a specific card of a player.

Rare: A scarce card or series of cards. Due to the term's subjectivity, it is currently used too liberally to popularize a card's value. When used on vintage cards, it can mean "hard to obtain" rather than available in limited quantities.

Rated Rookie: An original baseball term of a card that the *Donruss* Company used when designating a top-tier rookie player. It remains a part of the *Donruss'* hobby lexicon baseball brand of cards that *Panini* America owns.

Raw: A card that an authentication or grading company has not encapsulated.

Raw Card Review: A service that *Beckett Grading Services* offers at its onsite sports card shows. After examining a card, the company applies a number grade that seals the top loader of the card.

The encapsulation gives a collector an idea about the grade of a card. Notably, the *Raw Card Review* price is lower than that of a fully-graded card.

Re-colored/Re-Coloring: This is a fraudulent practice where one hides the physical damage or wear of a card using re-coloring techniques.

Redemption: This is a practice that multiple card manufacturers established to temporarily substitute a card that should be part of a product. The practice offers the right to redeem such a card when its manufacturer releases it.

The 2000s increased demand for autographed cards popularized the practice. However, the manufacturers left it to the athletes to return the contracted autographed cards. So, the manufacturers have to have to hold off the redemptions to await the return of the autographed cards.

Refractor: It is a card that uses a printing technology that enables it to refract and disperse light producing a rainbow-like effect. The increased demand for these types of cards has made them popular. *Topps* was the pioneering company in the use of the said printing technology.

Refractor Types: Because of the increasing popularity of the Refractor cards, there are several types of cards, and each set bears varying rarity degrees.

- *X-Fractor:* The second popular version after the regular version.
- *SuperFractor:* An ultra-rare or one-of-a-kind (1/1) card. It is highly valuable.

Release Date: The time when a new product of trading card becomes due for public availability. The unforeseen circumstance that the manufacturing process contains makes the release date fluid.

- *Street Date:* The date when a product becomes available in stores.

Repackaged Seller: The group case breaking growth in popularity made several companies spring up in the 2000s' second half. The occurrence coincided with the increased collector demand for higher-value trading cards of "hits."

Subsequently, companies that bought high-end cards from the secondary market repackaged them into new products. The Super Products is one of the most popular companies due to its line of Super Break brand products. The company is a branch of the California-based hobby shop, *South Bay Cards.*

Reprint: A deliberate replica of an original card. It is usually more expensive, whether in a set of single cards or not.

Retail Box: Sold in large retail chains and outlets, such as *Target.* There is variability between the contents of the two boxes. However, the Hobby Boxes have better insert odds or even different content altogether.

Recently, the retail outlets' buying power has given rise to a Retail Only products demand together with the products that have exclusive content.

- *Hobby Box:* A trading card box that traditional card shops and approved retailers sell exclusively.

Retail Only/Exclusive: Interchangeable terms referring to product, product configuration, and product content that retail channels distribute exclusively.

Rookie Card (RC): The first officially licensed trading card of a player after appearing on a major league level, including being in NHL, NBA, MLB, and NFL sports professional teams.

Rookie Premier/Rookie Showcase: An event that a specific players' association of a sport conducts to introduce newly drafted players to the media and trading card manufacturers.

- Rookie Premiere Autograph (RPA)
- Rookie Premier Signature (RPS)
- Rookie Premier Materials (RPM)

S

SASE (Self-Addressed Stamped Envelope): The collection of autographs via the TTM or mail.

Scarce: A scarce series of cards or card. The subjective term is currently used to popularize the value of a card. However, when used on vintage cards, scarce cards become more accessible to obtain than "rare" cards.

Secondary Market: An online marketplace, such as eBay.

Semi-High: A card belonging to the next-to-last series of an issued and numbered set. Its value is more than that of an average card but lower than that of a high number. A semi-high card has to have a corresponding premium.

Serial Number: A card of a specific quantity that bears a number sequence of xx/xxx (card number/quantity produced). It is meant for parallel cards, but "hits" and base cards also bear it currently. The card number on the upper left-hand corner is 4/5.

Series: Several cards belonging to a larger set. They are collectively released at a particular time. Until 1974, *Topps* was issuing cards that were in several series. The cards were released when the sports were in a regular session.

- High-Series, Semi-High, and High-Number.

Set: It is also referred to as the Base set.

Shill-bidding: An illegal activity where a seller increases their item's sale price through bidding for it. A seller can also engage a proxy to carry out the bidding.

Short-Print (SP): A base-set card with a lower printing quantity than other cards. Its production is out of necessity when manufacturers seek to spur additional sales when collectors pursue set completion.

Skip-Number: A major trading or sports card set with several un-issued cards featuring numbers between the lowest and the highest number that a set contains. Intentional and unintentional reasons of a trading card manufacturer give rise to a skip-number.

Slabbing/Slabbed: Protection of a card through encapsulation after grading and authentication. The protection is tamper-resistant.

Sports Card Album: A famous website that enables collectors to post their collection images and create an eBay list.

Sports Collectors Digest: A weekly publication for sports memorabilia collectors originally published by *Krause* and currently distributed by *F & W Media*.

Sports Marketing Report (SMR): A monthly hobby publication published by *Professional Sports Authenticators (PSA)*. It contains updates to the population reports for key cards.

Stand-Ups: A die-cut type of card that allowed the separation of the head of a player from the background section. One can make the card "stand up" by folding it in half. For example, the 1964 *Topps* Stand-up featuring Ernie Banks, the Hall of Famer from the Chicago Cubs.

Star Rookie: An *Upper Deck* term describing a potential young pro together with their *Upper Deck* card. It is used in football, basketball, and baseball cards.

Starting Lineup (SLU): An array of plastic action figures of sports athletes that *Kenner and Hasbro* manufactured in 1988-2001.

Sticker Autograph: An autograph signature on a label or sticker featured on a trading card.

Sticker Dump: A term collectors use to refer to a product with a liquidating purpose in the inventory of a trading company's surplus autograph stickers.

Subset: A themed number that trading cards have within the base set of a product. It can also be used to refer to as an insert set.

T

T.C.G. (Topps Gum Company): often appears on older sports cards and non-sports cards.

Team Bag: A storage plastic bag for trading cards. It has a sealed strip. It can host 25 cards. That is why it is referred to as a "team bag."

Team Card: A sports card showing a photo of a whole team.

Team Set: All cards featuring players of a specific team in a sports cards set.

Test Issue: Collectibles, such as trading cards, were released in the market for a trial exercise. *Topps* often used the practice. For example, in 1795, the company released the *Topps* minis on a trial basis. They remain highly sorted even today. The example below shows the 1967 *Topps* disc released only in Maryland.

Third-Party Services: Businesses affiliated with sports cards and memorabilia to provide support services to dealers, retailers, and collectors. The services include the provision of pricing information, image hosting, and card grading.

ThePit.com: A marketplace that allows trading sports cards as stock.

Tiffany Set: A *Topps* premium factory set, *Topps* traded, and Bowman sets produced in 1984-1991. Their quantities were smaller than that of the traditional sets. The premium white card stock was used to print the cards, and they had a coating of the glossy UV.

Tobacco Card: A card issued together with a cigarette pack. It was a marketing tool and a pack stabilizer that prevented the crushing of the cigarettes.

Top-Loader: A storage for single trading cards. It is a hard holder made of plastic. There are rigid and semi-rigid types that come in an array of density levels.

Traded Set: A set of trading cards featuring players, traded players, and called-up players in September from the minors. Their release was late into or past the regular season. They were issued in the factory form.

- *Update Sets, Updates, and Highlights:* The term replaced the term "Traded Set" to encompass the late-season sets. The replacement came due to the addition of cards featuring the statistical standout performances, record-breaking achievements, and post-season highlights.

Trading Card Game (TCG): It is a trading card used when playing a game.

- Collectible Card Game: Similar to the TCG.

Tuff Stuff: A no-longer-existing magazine that *Krause* used to print. It features all information regarding all entertainment and sports trading cards. It competed with *Beckett's* sports-specific magazines that required collectors to buy multiple magazines to get all the information about the cards.

U

Ultra-Pro: A company that manufactured collectibles, trading cards, storage supplies, and display units for the said items.

Uncut Sheet: A whole trading cards printed sheet that is yet to be cut into individual cards.

UV Coating: A layer that protects trading cards from fading due to exposure to the ultra-violet rays of the sun.

V

Variation (VAR): A unique card that stands out from the rest of the cards of the same set. The uniqueness can be in the form of color, letters, and photo variation. An example is the variations of the letter's color on the 1969 *Topps* baseball card of Mickey Mantle.

Vending Box: Trading cards in a box that were sold from a vending machine. Later, vendors started collating the boxes of cards into sets and selling them to the public. Each vending machine could host around 500 cards.

- *Vending Case:* Vending cases for wholesale distribution. Each contained 24 vending boxes equal to 12,000 cards.

Vintage: A subjective term referring to the entertainment and sports trading cards. Some people used it on anything printed before 1973, which was the year when *Topps* issued only a couple of series. Others use it for anything produced before 1970.

W

Want List: A list of designated cards that a collector reserves for his or her personal collection.

Wax: A general term for a box of packs or a single pack. It is a hobby vernacular term, even though manufacturers use different types of packaging.

Wax Pack: A wax-colored paper packaging used to pack and seal trading cards initially.

Wax Stain: Wax residue on top and bottom trading cards due to staying for an extended period without being opened.

Whale: Top customer(s) in a hobby shop in terms of spending when buying memorabilia, trading cards, or other inventory continuously. Such customers contribute to the overall sales revenue significantly.

White-Whale: A term that a collector created when describing an always-elusive card that belongs to their personal want list. It is a scarce and expensive card.

X

XRC: It is a term from the price guide publications. It designates a card of a player issued in their rookie year, but it does not belong to a standard base set. Such a card belongs to the 1980s, as well as the 1990s. It belonged to a limited edition that was traded or updated in the hobby during that period.

Y

Young Guns: An *Upper Deck* term describing a rookie card of a hockey player. The card is short-printed. It also holds its value for a long period, even without serial numbers or autographs. It is a rare card in the modern hobby world of sports card collecting.

How to get $98 worth of Sports Cards Research for Free

Free Bonus #1 ($49 value)

"7 Things You Must Do Before
Buying A Sports Card"

Free Bonus #2 ($49 value)

Our Custom Spreadsheet To Help You
Visualize The Price Trending And Projections
Of Your Favorite Sports Cards.

To get your Bonuses go to
https://betosalinas.activehosted.com/f/1

REFERENCES

2020 Panini Prizm football checklist, NFL set info, boxes, date, reviews. (2021, January 27). The Cardboard Connection. https://www.cardboardconnection.com/2020-panini-prizm-football-nfl-cards

admin. (n.d.). *How to increase eBay seller ratings—ListingMirror.* Listingmirror.com. https://www.listingmirror.com/blog/how-to-increase-ebay-seller-ratings/

Auctions, G. C. (2021, February 19). *PSA grading vs Beckett grading vs SGC grading (massive guide and review).* Https://Goldcardauctions.com/. https://goldcardauctions.com/psagrading-or-beckettgrading/#Beckett_Grading_Scale

Banker, T. (2020, April 16). *Retail Market Report | April 2020 | Sports Card Products to BUY or AVOID in Retail (Wal-Mart, Target, Dick's, & eBay).* BreakerCulture. https://breakerculture.com/retail-market-report-april-2020-sports-card-products-to-buy-or-avoid-in-retail-wal-mart-target-dicks-ebay/

Bartsch, T. (2019, March 6). *Quotable: Athletes commenting on cards, autographs.* Sports Collectors Digest. https://sportscollectorsdigest.com/cards/quotable-athletes-commenting-on-cards-autographs

Breakout Sports Cards. (2020, September 11). *What brand of sports cards are the most valuable* - Breakoutsportscards.com. https://breakoutsportscards.com/tips/what-brand-of-sports-cards-are-the-most-valuable/

Cali, A. (2019, October 21). *Chasing the rainbow: The challenge & satisfaction of collecting parallels*. Beckett News. https://www.beckett.com/news/chasing-rainbow-collecting-parallels/

Cardboard Connection. (n.d.). *Trading card manufacturers*. The Cardboard Connection. https://www.cardboardconnection.com/brand

Check out my baseball cards, comics & collectibles. (2012). Comc.com. https://www.comc.com/

Collier, M. (n.d.-a). *How to find sold items on eBay*. Dummies. https://www.dummies.com/business/online-business/ebay/how-to-find-sold-items-on-ebay/

Collier, M. (n.d.-b). *Read eBay item descriptions carefully*. Dummies. https://www.dummies.com/business/online-business/ebay/read-ebay-item-descriptions-carefully/

Cracknell, R. (2017, February 6). *2017 Topps baseball parallels gallery and details*. Beckett News. https://www.beckett.com/news/2017-topps-baseball-parallels/

Cracknell, R. (2019, December 13). *2019-20 Panini prizm basketball prizms parallels rainbow gallery, guide*. Beckett News. https://www.beckett.com/news/2019-20-panini-prizm-basketball-prizms-rainbow/

David, P. (2020, February 6). *Secret criteria to know what to buy for sports card investing*. Sports Card Investor. https://www.sportscardinvestor.com/2020/02/06/secret-criteria-to-know-what-to-buy-for-sports-card-investing/

Dunne, C. (2019, April 8). *7 ways to get more eBay feedback—FeedbackExpress*. FeedbackExpress. https://www.feedbackexpress.com/7-ways-get-ebay-feedback/

eBay standard envelope. (n.d.). EBay Standard Envelope. https://pages.ebay.com/ebaystandardenvelope/index.html

Elliot, J. (2020, August 20). *Finding your "why" in the hobby*. Sports Card Investor. https://www.sportscardinvestor.com/2020/08/20/finding-your-why-in-the-hobby/

GO GTS Distribution. (n.d.). *Sports card collecting 101: Glossary of sports cards terms and definitions—Go GTS*. Go GTS Distribution. https://gogts.net/sports-card-collecting-101-glossary-of-sports-cards-terms-and-definitions/

Goss, N. (n.d.). *15 most valuable hockey cards of all-time*. Bleacher Report. https://bleacherreport.com/articles/812055-nhl-the-15-most-valuable-hockey-cards-of-all-time

GTS Distribution. (n.d.). *History of Bowman baseball cards—Go GTS*. GTS Distribution. https://gogts.net/history-of-bowman-baseball-cards/

Loff, S. (2020, May 14). *SGC vs. PSA: A study weighing your options as a collector*. Sports Card Investor. https://www.sportscardinvestor.com/2020/05/14/sgc-vs-psa-a-study-weighing-your-options-as-a-collector/

Lukas, P. (2019, February 25). *What do we think of Jersey Trading Cards?* Uni Watch. https://uni-watch.com/2019/02/25/what-do-we-think-of-jersey-trading-cards/

Melia, T. (2020, May 14). *Factors that impact trading card value*. PSA Blog. https://blog.psacard.com/2020/05/14/factors-that-impact-trading-card-value/

Memorabilia Displays. (2020, July 28). *What drives the value of sports memorabilia?* Memorabilia Displays. https://memorabiliadisplays.com/blogs/hobby-news/what-drives-the-value-of-sports-memorabilia

Michel, P. (2020, April 30). *The overnight explosion of base cards.* Sports Card Investor. https://www.sportscardinvestor.com/2020/04/30/the-overnight-explosion-of-base-cards/

North Star Alliance. (2018). *What is "box breaking?" | Northstar Problem Gambling Alliance.* Northstarpg.org. https://www.northstarpg.org/2018/06/what-is-box-breaking/

Olds, C. (2014, December 12). *The List: 50 group-breakers to know.* Beckett News. https://www.beckett.com/news/the-list-50-group-breakers-to-know/

Orlando, J. (n.d.). *Ten tips for building a collection.* Psacard.com. https://www.psacard.com/articles/articleview/6315/ten-tips-building-collection

Ortega, S. (2020, January 22). *Are you a collector or are you an investor?* Sports Card Investor. https://www.sportscard-investor.com/2020/01/22/are-you-a-collector-or-are-you-an-investor/

Osborne, A. J. (2020, May 19). *Set building 101.* SABR's Baseball Cards Research Committee. https://sabrbase-ballcards.blog/2020/05/19/set-building-101/

Peng, S. (2020, November 17). *Most expensive baseball cards ever sold.* Www.stadiumtalk.com. https://www.stadiumtalk.com/s/most-expensive-baseball-cards-985687df1bbe45c5

Pre-war Cards. (2019, January 29). *Team sets are an idea as old as card collecting itself.* Pre-War Cards. https://prewar-cards.com/2019/01/29/team-sets-are-an-idea-as-old-as-card-collecting-itself/

PSA Collector. (n.d.). *Best way to submit your cards to the PSA for grading 2018.* Psacollector.com. https://www.psacollector.com/best-way-to-submit-your-cards-to-psa-for-grading-2018/

PWCC announces a new research tool available to the public. (2018, June 29). Www.businesswire.com. https://www.

businesswire.com/news/home/20180629005043/en/PWCC-Announces-New-Research-Tool-Available-to-the-Public

Ransom, M. (2020, October 15). *The secrets of discord.* Sports Card Investor. https://www.sportscardinvestor.com/2020/10/15/the-secrets-of-discord/

Seideman, D. (2018, September 19). *Tech entrepreneur determines first estimate of U.S. sports memorabilia market: $5.4 billion.* Forbes. https://www.forbes.com/sites/davidseideman/2018/09/19/tech-entrepreneur-determines-first-true-estimate-of-sports-memorabilia-market-5-4-billion/?sh=31c792a552e8

Simple, secure shipping for trading cards. (2020, December 11). Community.ebay.com. https://community.ebay.com/t5/Announcements/Simple-Secure-Shipping-for-Trading-Cards/ba-p/31420436

Sports Card Investor. (2020). BIG NEWS: eBay Seller Protections & New Shipping Options in 2021 [YouTube Video]. In *YouTube.* https://www.youtube.com/watch?v=Q3LkIEEVwg8

Sports cards: New release calendar list, checklist, guide, dates, boxes. (n.d.). The Cardboard Connection. https://www.cardboardconnection.com/new-release-calender

StockX mobile app | iOS. (2016). Stockx.com. https://stockx.com/how-it-works

The history and value of collecting sports cards. (n.d.). Robscollectibles.com. http://robscollectibles.com/collecting-sportscards.html

The most valuable football cards of all time. (2019, June 12). All Vintage Cards. https://allvintagecards.com/most-valuable-football-cards/

The Panini Group. (n.d.). *Panini United Kingdom: The Panini Group*. Collectibles.panini.co.uk. https://collectibles.panini.co.uk/company/the-panini-group.html

ThePit : Welcome to ThePit.com. (n.d.). Thepit.com. https://thepit.com/

Torrey, J. (2020a, July 12). *How big is the market for sports cards*. Sports Card Investor. https://www.sportscardinvestor.com/2020/07/12/how-big-is-the-market-for-sports-cards/

Torrey, J. (2020b, October 25). *How to properly check Ebay comps*. Sports Card Investor. https://www.sportscardinvestor.com/2020/10/25/how-to-properly-check-ebay-comps/

Trading card analytics tool | PWCC Marketplace. (n.d.). Www.pwccmarketplace.com. https://www.pwccmarketplace.com/market-price-research

Trading card grading. (n.d.). Professional Sports Authenticator (PSA). https://www.psacard.com/services/tradingcardgrading

Upper deck sports | Tips on collecting—The differences in Sets & card types. (n.d.). Sports.upperdeck.com. http://sports.upperdeck.com/collectorszone/tips/tips_setcardtypes.aspx?visited=1

Vaynerchuk, G. (1970a, January 1). *9 factors to consider before buying sports cards*. GaryVaynerchuk.com. https://www.garyvaynerchuk.com/9-factors-to-consider-before-investing-in-sports-cards/

Vaynerchuk, G. (1970b, January 1). *Why I believe sports cards are about to explode in culture and value*. GaryVaynerchuk.com. https://www.garyvaynerchuk.com/sports-cards-value-will-explode/

Whaley, A. (2019, August 18). *Player collecting has its rewards and its pitfalls*. Sports Collectors Daily. https://www.sportscollectorsdaily.com/player-collecting-has-its-rewards-and-its-pitfalls/

What years are vintage baseball cards? (n.d.). All Vintage Cards. https://allvintagecards.com/what-years-vintage-baseball-cards/

(2021). Blowoutforums.com. https://www.blowoutforums.com/showthread.php?t=662826